DONALD J. JOHNSON

TWISTED UNTO DESTRUCTION

How "Bible Alone" Theology
Made the World a Worse Place

Catholic
Answers
Press

All Scripture citations taken from the Revised Standard Version Second Catholic Edition.

Published by Catholic Answers, Inc.

2020 Gillespie Way

El Cajon, California 92020

1-888-291-8000 orders

619-387-0042 fax

catholic.com

Printed in the United States of America

Cover design by eBookLaunch.com

Interior design by Russell Graphic Design

978-1-68357-275-6

978-1-68357-276-3 Kindle

978-1-68357-277-0 ePub

ACKNOWLEDGMENTS

Getting a book published is always a huge team effort, and there are too many people who have supported this project to mention here, but I do want to say a special thanks to everyone at Catholic Answers for seeing the vision and getting behind this book. Also, thanks to Todd Aglialoro and Drew Belsky for your extraordinary editing abilities. Finally, thanks to Carl Olson for all the great conversations and feedback. This wouldn't have been possible without all of you.

CONTENTS

SCRIPTURE-TWISTING IN THE LAST DAYS

A lmost 2,000 years ago, the apostle Paul wrote to his young apprentice Timothy about the terrible times to come: "For men will be lovers of self, lovers of money, proud, arrogant, abusive, disobedient to their parents, ungrateful, unholy, inhuman, implacable, slanderers, profligates, fierce, haters of good, treacherous, reckless, swollen with conceit, lovers of pleasure rather than lovers of God" (2 Tim. 3:2–4). Doesn't it feel as if Paul were speaking directly to twenty-first-century America? It's as if he had entered a time machine and were scrolling through Twitter and Facebook (and scanning the most popular shows on Netflix). America is a mess, and I think Paul's vice-filled description sums it up nicely.

Sadly, it's not just the secular world. American Christianity is an ethical disaster, too. If you've seen the reports of abuse and corruption,[1] or perhaps just interacted with individual Christians (especially online), then you'll know already what sociological research has confirmed: for the most part, the moral practices of American Christians are essentially the same as those of non-Christians.[2] As Michael Horton laments: "Christians are as likely to embrace life-styles every bit as hedonistic, materialistic, self-centered, and sexually immoral as the world in general."[3]

That wouldn't be news to Paul. In the next line of the passage quoted above, Paul continues his description of the Last Days by characterizing the people as "holding the form of religion but denying the power of it." The sinful people he's talking about are Christians! (Or, at least, people who claim the label.) Unfortunately, these believers have a "corrupt mind" and practice a "counterfeit faith" (2 Tim. 3:8). They are deceived and are deceiving others.

Paul wasn't the only apostle writing about this. St. Peter speaks of the end times in a similar manner in the third chapter of his second letter. He notes that the Last Days will be filled with "scoffers" and "lawless men" who "follow their own evil desires" rather than God's righteous decrees. Sadly, these men also masquerade as true believers. Indeed, they are using Scripture to support their sinful ways! Peter closes his letter by pointing out that some passages in the Bible, Paul's letters especially, are "hard to understand" and subject to being misinterpreted. He encourages his readers not to get carried away by false teachers, "ignorant and unstable" people who take Scripture and "twist" it, "as they do the other scriptures." These evildoers will not be prepared, Peter warns, for the "day of the Lord," which will come "like a thief" and bring judgment on the earth. They will have twisted Scripture "to their own destruction" (2 Pet. 3:1–18).

2 TIM 3:16
2 TIM 3:15
2 TIM 4:3-4

How are we to avoid a similar fate? According to Paul, the answer is to understand and use Scripture properly. Earlier in his letter, he had already admonished Timothy to be a workman who does not need to be ashamed before God, but who correctly handles the word of truth (2 Tim. 2:15). Then, after describing the Last Days, Paul lays out a battle plan for Timothy by commanding him to "preach the word," because "all scripture is inspired by God and profitable for reproof, for correction, and for training in righteousness, that the man of God may be complete, equipped for every good work" (3:16). As Timothy uses Scripture to "convince, rebuke, and exhort," he will be attempting to counteract the evil done by false teachers, because "the time is coming when people will not endure sound teaching, but having itching ears they will accumulate for themselves teachers to suit their own likings, and will turn away from listening to the truth and wander into myths" (4:3–4).

The overarching problem here is that we have a bunch of ostensibly religious people using Scripture for nefarious ends. They are abandoning true doctrines and replacing them with allegedly scriptural teachings they are more comfortable with—teachings that allow them to exhibit the sinful characteristics listed above. The solution is to set them straight using Scripture in the proper way.

The Bible Alone Is Not Enough

So far so good, right? I doubt that many American Christians, of whatever variety, would disagree with anything I've said so far. However, my next statement, which I will support and expand upon in this book, is sure to be more controversial: Protestantism, with its doctrine of *sola scriptura*, is incapable of properly implementing Paul's instructions to Timothy. That

11

is to say, the Bible alone, used apart from any interpretive or ecclesial authority, simply cannot adequately fight the misuse of Scripture and moral decay described by Peter and Paul. Not only that, but *sola scriptura* ultimately makes the moral situation worse by creating a culture of moral relativism and even providing a divine mandate for sin. In other words, not only can Protestantism's approach to Scripture *not* fix the evil faced by the New Testament writers, but it actually causes and exacerbates that evil, and always has.

Before turning to the evidence for that claim, a quick note: In the chapters that follow, I will be presenting evidence that *sola scriptura*, as a philosophy of divine revelation, simply doesn't provide an objective basis for morality. *I am not saying individual Protestant believers cannot be moral based on their understanding of Scripture.* Of course they can. I was an Evangelical Protestant for most of my life, and almost all of my immediate family members and friends are Evangelical Protestants. I know that Evangelical Protestants can be personally holy. This has nothing to do with whether or not you can read the Bible and use it to increase in holiness. However, what I *am* saying is that individual Protestants are doing this in spite of the weaknesses of their system, not because of the strengths of their system.

It's sort of like discussing morality with atheists. When I point out to atheists that an atheistic worldview, which asserts that matter is all that exists, does not leave room for any objective standard of right and wrong,[4] the response is often, "What are you saying, that I can't be good without God? That all atheists are wicked?" No, that is not what I am saying. On the contrary, atheists can be good people—but, like Protestants, atheists who practice righteousness are doing it in spite of the weakness of their worldview, not because of its strength. Atheism is not the worldview to promote for a righteous culture, as the history of officially atheistic regimes can attest.[5]

A similar principle applies to Protestantism. Ultimately, if you want to produce a truly righteous culture on a wide scale, Protestantism is not the worldview to promote. It simply does not have the philosophical and theological foundation to handle the job. The history of Protestantism, particularly as it has been lived out in America, attests to that. To that story we now turn.

CHAPTER 1

THE BIBLE...
ALONE?

I grew up in a family centered on the Bible. My father graduated from a Bible institute, preached at a Bible church, and directed a Bible camp in the summers. As a family we hosted Bible studies, watched Bible videos, attended Bible conferences, hung Bible art on the wall, and memorized thousands of Bible verses. The Bible was the air we breathed.

The reason I was so immersed in the Bible is that we were Evangelical Protestants who believed in the doctrine of *sola scriptura*. That is to say, we considered the Bible our sole infallible source of faith and practice. In other words, we were convinced that Scripture is the only way to know God and that everything we needed to understand him and our faith could be attained simply by picking up the Bible and reading it. So we did. And frankly, the scriptural foundation with which I was raised has been an incredible blessing. I am so thankful for my parents and my upbringing.

Interestingly, though, even with all the Bible I learned, my scriptural education was not without gaps and weaknesses. For example, we never learned Bible history. I don't mean the history recorded in the Bible; we knew those stories well. I mean that we never studied the history of the book itself, or where we got the notion of *sola scriptura*. Instead, we simply took for granted what I now realize were vague, unsupported propositions that we didn't really understand.

For example, we believed firmly that "God gave us the Bible." But what did that mean, and how had he done that? No one ever said. As a child, I assumed he dropped it from the sky or sent it in the mail. As I grew older and learned a bit more about who wrote the books of Scripture, I envisioned scriptural authors as old men in a trance, writing down words as God spoke through a megaphone from heaven. But I didn't really know how we got the book, and I never really thought deeply about it. Nor did any of my Sunday school teachers, apparently. As Scripture-centered as my upbringing was, it wasn't until I got into Bible college (one more!) that I was ever even presented with the topic of the origin and transmission of the sacred text.

Also, we believed that we didn't need any outside interpretive authority to tell us God's truth; God revealed his truth to everyone directly through the Bible alone, and the Bible was its own authority. Well, at least that is what we claimed. In reality, we all knew that the Bible is incredibly confusing and hard to understand, which is why we needed all those teachers at the Bible churches, colleges, camps, and conferences. They were our interpretive authority. But we would never have admitted that, or even have been able to articulate it. We clung tightly to the idea that the Bible spoke for itself and did not need outside authorities to understand it. Where did we get that idea? We didn't know, and I don't remember anyone ever asking. And how did we reconcile that claim with our practice of always trusting someone else to interpret Scripture for us? I don't remember anyone ever trying. Nor did anyone ever try to explain what happened at the Reformation. It may seem strange, considering that it is the thing from which Protestants draw their name and religious identity ("Protesting" the Catholic Church), but most American Protestants have a limited understanding of Church history, including the Reformation. I was not at all different. I had a vague notion that Luther and the other Reformers had done something to save Christianity from the corrupt Catholic Church and bring it "back to the Bible alone," but I had no real idea what that meant or what actually happened. Neither do most Protestants today. For the most part, they simply don't do history.

I bring this up because when I did start researching the history of the Bible, the Church, and the Reformation, I realized that this gap in my Bible-centered life was no small oversight. In fact, even with all of the blessings of my Scripture-saturated youth, my ignorance had kept me from receiving much of what the Bible, and the Christian faith as a whole, has to offer.[6]

It had also kept me from being as strong as I could have been in fighting moral relativism. Like many of my Evangelical peers, I have long tried to maintain what I consider a "biblical" witness against our culture's embrace of sins such as abortion, sexual immorality, racism, and rampant materialism. However, it didn't seem as though any of us was making any headway. As I studied Church history and the effects of the Reformation, I realized why.

In this chapter, we will go over a brief history of the doctrine of *sola scriptura* and see how it resulted in doctrinal relativism. In the chapters that follow, we will see how that doctrinal relativism played out in moral relativism, to the great detriment of millions of lives.

The Reformation

Martin Luther was in a bind. His attempt at reforming the Church had met stiff resistance, and now he was in an argument with the clerical authorities over how to understand salvation. Does God *make* people righteous in salvation, or does he only *label* them righteous? Luther taught the latter, and the Church ruled that he was promoting false doctrine in doing so.

To reject their decision was to reject the authority of the Church, which Luther was prepared to do. However, that left him with a problem. On what basis could he support his new theology? He couldn't just stand up and say, "I know better than the Church about God's plan of salvation because God has spoken directly to me and given me superior wisdom and insight." He would have been either ignored or laughed off the stage of history, at least at that point in time. Instead, he defended his beliefs by saying his authority was not the Catholic Church and its understanding of Scripture, but Scripture alone: "I consider myself convicted by the testimony of Holy Scripture, which is my basis: my conscience is captive to the Word of God. Thus I cannot and will not recant . . . God help me!"

It sounded great, and people ate it up. But it is important to realize that Luther's appeal to a new epistemological standard for theology resulted from his getting backed into a corner, not because he suddenly discovered (or rediscovered) a truth that had been hidden since the early Church. He wasn't reading through the Bible one day when the proposition that "the Bible is the only authority" suddenly jumped out at him. So his "discovery" was not *sola scriptura*, but rather the new doctrine of *forensic justification*.[7] *Sola scriptura* was then, reflexively, understood and taught as the means by which he got the teaching about justification.[8] He needed a competing authority to pit against the Catholic Church, and *sola scriptura* fit that role. But *sola scriptura* was not part of Luther's original objection to the Church, nor was it on his mind when he began his quest to reform the Church. Perhaps if it had been, he would have thought through the consequences a little more seriously.

Doctrinal Chaos

Sola scriptura dictates that no person or institution can speak for God; all we have are words on a page, and they speak for themselves.

The problem is that words on a page simply don't speak for themselves. They must be interpreted. There is simply no way around this: every act of reading Scripture is simultaneously an act of interpreting Scripture. What *sola scriptura* means in practice, then, is not "the Bible alone as an authority for faith and morals," but "someone's interpretation of the Bible as the authority for faith and morals." As everyone who has ever sat in a small-group Bible study knows, this leads to disagreements. Because there is no outside interpretive authority to which to appeal for guidance, these disagreements are impossible to resolve. That is why, from the beginning of the Reformation, Protestants broke up into splinter groups based on divergent readings of the same texts from the same Bible.

For example, many of Luther's close friends and fellow theologians quickly disagreed with him on the interpretation of a variety of texts. Perhaps the most famous example is the battle over the correct interpretation of 1 Corinthians 11:23–24, the passage in which Jesus institutes the Eucharist. "The Lord Jesus on the night he was betrayed took bread, and when he had given thanks he broke it and said, 'This is my body which is for you. Do this in remembrance of me.'"

What did Jesus mean when he said, "This is my body"? To Luther, the answer couldn't have been clearer: Jesus was saying the bread of the Eucharist is indeed the real presence of Christ. Uldrich Zwingli, however, interpreted Jesus' words more symbolically. Zwingli denied *transubstantiation*, the traditional notion that the substance of the elements change and literally become the body and blood of Christ, and instead taught that the Lord's Supper was a memorial ceremony. For Zwingli, Jesus gave us the Lord's Supper as more of an object lesson, a psychological tool to help us focus on Jesus' sacrifice.

Zwingli was not alone in rejecting Luther's interpretation. Between 1525 and 1527, at least eight other Reformers published over twenty-five treatises against Luther's view of the Eucharist.[9] This debate was causing so much dissension that Philip I of Hessen organized a colloquy in Marburg to come to an agreement on the question. It proved undoable. Even though Luther and Zwingli were reading the exact same Bible with the exact same passages of Scripture, they came to different conclusions, and because they did not acknowledge any outside interpretive authority to which they must submit, no solution was possible. Even calling a formal meeting to discuss the issue was no use. Indeed, the division between the two men was never solved, and it remains one of the main dividing lines between "Lutheran" and "Reformed" strands of Protestantism.

Notice how different this is from the way the Catholic Church has always dealt with these issues. From the beginning of Christianity, there have been doctrinal disagreements and arguments over the interpretation of particular Scripture passages. However, the Catholic Church has never attempted to solve them by scheduling leaderless colloquies. Rather, the Church calls councils. From the Council of Jerusalem in Acts 15, the Church has dealt with disputes by bringing the leaders of the Church together and, after prayer and discussion, making a pronouncement that settles the issue.

For example, in the third century, a dispute arose about the nature of Jesus' divinity. A priest from Egypt named Arius began teaching that Jesus had been created by God the Father at a particular point in time. Arius was opposed by Athanasius of Alexandria, who insisted that Jesus had always existed as part of the Godhead. Who was right? Believe it or not, most of the general public sided with Arius. However, doctrine is not a matter of popular opinion or individual interpretation in the Catholic Church, so the pope called the Council of Nicaea in 325 and condemned Arianism as a heresy. That decision is still announced every day around the world when people recite the Nicene Creed.

No such clarity is possible within the framework of Scripture alone. As such, the doctrinal disagreements unleashed by the Protestant Reformation multiplied. One of the most contentious involved infant baptism. Although major Reformers such as Luther, Zwingli, and John Calvin supported and defended the traditional practice of baptizing babies, to Swiss theologian Conrad Grebel, it was a senseless, blasphemous abomination against all Scripture."[10] This sentiment was echoed by Felix Manz, who declared the baptizing of babies "against God, an insult to Christ, and a trampling underfoot of his own true, eternal word."[11]

If you know anything about Martin Luther, you know he wasn't going to take that charge quietly. Luther could hurl insults with the best of them, and he was clear that he considered those who disagreed with him on doctrine stooges of the devil and bound for hell. For example, although he agreed with Zwingli on almost every issue except the Eucharist, after the Marburg Colloquy, Luther considered Zwingli a non-Christian who would be damned. He warned his readers to "beware of Zwingli and avoid his books as the hellish poison of Satan, for the man is completely perverted and has completely lost Christ."[12] When Zwingli was killed in a battle, Luther believed that it was a punishment from God for being an infidel.[13]

Luther treated the Anabaptists Grebel and Manz the same way. In his *Letter to the Christians of Antwerp*, he explains that Satan's new strategy is to inhabit the "ungodly" and get them to interpret Scripture falsely:

> This one will not hear of baptism, that one denies the sacrament, another puts a world between this and the Last Day: some teach that Christ is not God, some say this, some say that: there are about as many sects and creeds as there are heads. No yokel is so rude, but when he has dreams and fancies, he thinks himself inspired by the Holy Ghost and must be a prophet.[14]

What Luther is describing here is not demonic possession, but the doctrinal relativism that is the logical result of *sola scriptura*. His letter gives us insight into how Protestants were trying to deal with the chaos. Rather than admit that *sola scriptura*, by its nature, leads to disagreements in interpretation, they invoked the Holy Spirit as the one who would guide them in all truth and make sure their interpretations were correct.

This did not help at all. First, it did nothing to quell doctrinal relativism. There were still just as many different interpretations of Scripture, but now each interpreter believed he had the Holy Spirit ensuring that his interpretation was correct. "What am I to do," asked Dutch philosopher Erasmus in 1524, "when many persons allege different interpretations, each one of whom swears to have the Spirit?"[15] Good question. As Reformation-era historian Brad Gregory points out, few, if any, responded to a contrary opinion by changing his mind. I can find no examples of one debater saying to the other, "You're right: I lack the Holy Spirit's guidance in my reading of Scripture, and I see that you have it in yours. I admit I was mistaken, so I'll trust you instead." Rather, most were like Zwingli, who wrote, "I know for certain that God teaches me, because I have experienced it."[16]

This leads to the second consequence: invoking the Holy Spirit made the situation worse in that it caused people to dig in and fight even harder for what they were convinced was true. After all, if God is your personal teacher, he is on your side. How, then, could you back down from those who disagree with you? They are obviously enemies of God. As such, theological debates among Protestants during the time of the Reformation were given a cosmic weight, sometimes even becoming life-and-death struggles. Manz, for example, was condemned to death by Zwingli and a group of his fellow Reformers for performing an adult baptism in Zurich.[17] He became the first of many who would lose their lives in what became known as the "Radical Reformation," the continued splintering of Protestant groups as they rebelled against the original rebels.[18]

That splintering never ended. *Sola scriptura* means that every preacher with an opinion and the ability to gain followers has the potential to start a new religious group, and that is exactly what has happened in the centuries since. Some of the more successful innovators have included John Knox (founder of the Presbyterians), George Fox (Quakers), Menno Simons (Mennonites), Robert Brown (Congregationalists), Michaelis Jones (Dutch Reformed), John and Charles Wesley (Methodists), and Theophilus Lindley (Unitarians), not to mention the innumerable leaders within the various Baptist and Pentecostal denominations. Within each of these broad groups are dozens, if not hundreds, of other splinter groups.

Protestants found fertile ground for expansion, and more division, in the New World. With its lack of Catholics and attitude of religious freedom, formally adopted in the establishment clause of the First Amendment, America provided an opportunity to see what *sola scriptura* could look like in its purest form yet.

The result has been predictable. The various Protestant groups have continued to splinter over everything from style of government to style of music, with theological disagreements over everything from salvation to speaking in tongues. As French emigrant Achille Murat observed in 1832, America has "a thousand and one sects which divide the people. . . . Merely to enumerate them would be impossible, for they change every day, appear, disappear, unite, separate, and evince nothing stable but their instability."[19]

That's why many towns in America have a "Church Street" that contains a First Baptist, Second Baptist, and Third Baptist Church, along with a Fourth Presbyterian, a Conservative Lutheran (to contrast with the Evangelical Lutheran) and two "Churches of Christ." That last one is particularly ironic in that the Church of Christ (or *Christian Church*) movement was started to restore unity in the Church. There are now several brands of Christian Church in America, as the movement has split several times over the years. Founded in order to end denominationalism, it has now itself become several denominations.

That is also why so many new forms of "Christianity" have been founded in America. To cite just one historical example, in just a few short years at the beginning of the nineteenth century, one section of New York State produced so many new "revivals" and emotionally exciting religious movements that it became known as the Burned-Over District. Leaders from that brief period who were convinced that they were finally preaching the one true form of Christianity included William Miller (Jehovah's Witnesses and Seventh Day Adventists), the Fox Sisters (Plymouth Spiritualism), John Humphrey Noyes (The Oneida Community), and Joseph Smith (Mormonism).

Things haven't really changed that much. Indeed, in the week I am writing this, a group of Southern Baptists (more on how they became "southern" in the next chapter) have been fighting over whether to allow women to preach. As always, the debate is over the proper interpretation of Scripture, and this tweet from Pastor Grant Castleberry would have fit right in during the Reformation: "Some things are so clear in Scripture that to deny them is to deny Scripture itself. To change 'I do not permit a woman to teach or exercise authority over a man' to 'I DO permit' is not a mere misinterpretation but a denial of the full inspiration & sufficiency of Scripture."[20]

Really? A quick glance at the replies to this tweet will confirm what we already know: the Bible isn't nearly as clear to everyone else as it seems to Pastor Castleberry. How do we decide the correct position? Within *sola scriptura*, there simply is no way. Will those congregants who disagree with this pastor change their position because of what he said? Not likely. Most will simply pack up and leave, either to find a group that agrees with them, or to start their own.

Interestingly, those entrepreneurial types who start their own communities no longer usually openly affiliate with any larger denomination. Since *sola scriptura* is all about denying the authority of tradition, with each new generation, that anti-tradition principle keeps getting played farther out to its logical end. Today, that means abandoning any semblance of traditional ties to other Protestant denominations or even the Reformation itself. Now the breakaway groups use names like "Lakewood Bible Church" or "Hilltop Community Church." Some even get rid of the "Church" label altogether. "Hey, neighbor, want to go with me to 'Renovation' this weekend?" In reality, these get-togethers should be called "a group that likes the teaching of [insert name of pastor here]," because that is ultimately what they are. The bottom line is that the preaching is the only reason most congregants attend. As soon as they disagree with the teaching, they'll depart. If their favorite pastor moves on, so will they.

That is all related to what happened at the Reformation. When the Bible alone became the source of faith and morals, the pulpit literally replaced the altar at the center of the church,[21] and preaching replaced the Eucharist as the primary reason to attend. Because each person is ultimately his own authority on the Bible, people "shop" for a place where the pastor teaches the Bible in a way that they agree with. You might even say these folks "accumulate for themselves teachers to suit their own likings" (2 Tim. 4:3).

Ironically, I believe that this is one under-reported reason why attendance at Christian churches is declining, even among those who consider themselves believers. With the advent of technology that allows people to hear or watch a sermon without attending services, it is much harder for Protestants to give compelling reasons for folks to attend. Many Christians now follow their favorite preachers by subscribing to podcasts and YouTube channels; why should they have to get up early on a Sunday morning and drive somewhere when they can get "church" in on the commute to work each day?[22]

To add to that point, think about the type of "preaching" that these "parishioners" are consuming. These days, it might not come from the pastor of a congregation at all. Indeed, many of the most popular Bible teachers now are armchair theologians, offering weekly or daily ruminations on YouTube and Instagram from their cars or home offices. They are solo ministry entrepreneurs, without any connection to a larger denominational group.

So the splintering of the Church due to *sola scriptura* has almost succeeded in doing away with groups altogether. Luther once mentioned to his friend Melanchthon that the Reformation made every person "his own rabbi."[23] With the advent of the internet and the iPhone, now every person is not only his own rabbi, but his own church, and the journey to absolute doctrinal chaos seems almost complete.

Moral Chaos

That path doesn't end with *religious* hyper-individualism. It also leads to *moral* hyper-individualism. Theological relativism goes with ethical relativism, as each person gets to decide for himself not only what he thinks about God, but what he believes is right and wrong. After all, if God is the standard for goodness, but we know him only through the Bible, and therefore we can't agree about what God is like or what he wants, we won't be able to agree about good and evil, either.

We've already mentioned how this has played out in the disputes over baptism and women's role in ministry. Other historical spats include disagreements over drinking, dancing, and smoking. I remember the first time I met a good Christian family that drank alcohol. It blew my mind! After growing up in an Evangelical culture in which drinking was a sin, I was shocked that these folks didn't see a problem with a glass of wine at dinner or a beer with their barbecue. What Bible were they reading? Well, the same one I was, and with a much stronger exegetical approach than I had, as it turns out. Looking back, I chuckle at our attempts to defend teetotaling from the Bible. "In Bible days, the 'wine' wasn't fermented—it was just plain grape juice," I was taught. Good grief.

Other moral debates are no laughing matter. In the rest of the book, we are going to cover some of the more serious moral consequences of Protestantism. As renowned Irish academic George O'Brien explains in *The Economic Effects of the Reformation*, that religious revolution unleashed moral chaos in every area of life by untethering ethics from the Church: "From the moment that the Reformers proclaimed the right of resistance to authority by establishing private judgment as a dogma, Christian morality remained without support, as there was no longer any authority recognized as entitled to explain and teach it."[24] As such, sin increased.

Even Luther recognized this fact, and he constantly complained about Protestants' moral laxity. In one passage, he wrote, "Our people are seven times more scandalous than others have ever been up to this. We steal, we lie, we deceive, we eat and drink to excess, and we give ourselves to every vice."[25] He also noted, "We now see the people becoming more infamous, more avaricious, more merciless, more unchaste, and in every way worse than they are under the papacy."[26] Fellow Protestant leader Joachim Camerarius complained that "mankind have now attained the goal of their desires—boundless liberty to think and act exactly as they please. Reason, moderation, law, morality, and duty have all lost their value."[27]

The Reformation unleashed not just moral relativism and confusion; it also provided people a way to give moral evils a divine mandate. That is to say, *sola scriptura* opened the door not only for more sin, but for sin to be justified in the name of God. As we will see, the Bible alone as an authority leads to "the Bible tells me I can do this thing that used to be considered a sin."

In the pages that follow, we will examine this phenomenon in history, especially as it has played out in America with regard to three major areas of vice: power, money, and sex. Chapter 2 deals with the lust for power, exemplified in America's history with racism. Chapter 3 is about love of money as displayed in rampant consumerism. Chapter 4 tells the story of the ongoing Sexual Revolution, particularly as it relates to contraception.

I have three main objectives for each chapter:

1. Examine the nature of the evil in question, and briefly explain why the Church has always opposed it. I will also show how these sins rose to prominence in our culture, focusing on a few of the major historical figures and events that accelerated the acceptance of each vice.

2. Survey how Protestants dealt with each issue, and show how in each case, the Bible alone has not been enough to stem the tide of immorality. Indeed, as we will see, in each case, *sola scriptura* has exacerbated the problem by giving each sin a "biblical" stamp of approval, entrenching these evils into American culture and leading millions to pain, sorrow, and ultimately destruction.

3. Contrast that with the Catholic approach, pointing out a few of the ways that the Catholic Church has fought the rise of these evils and what it is doing to stand strong today.

CHAPTER 2

AMERICA'S ORIGINAL SIN

In August 1619, a slave ship captained by Manuel Mendes da Cunha carried 350 Africans toward Vera Cruz, New Spain. Before it arrived, Captain Cunha's ship was attacked and robbed by an English corsair that then sold about twenty of those Africans in Virginia. It was the first recorded transaction of its kind in the colonies, and thus began slavery in what would become the United States of America.

Made in the Image of God

When the first Africans were sold in the colonies, conscience and tradition gave at least some of the locals pause. Should we really be buying and selling other human beings? Isn't that against the Faith? The Catholic Church certainly taught that it was. Although many Catholics were slave traders, and many American Catholics would end up owning slaves, the official teaching of the Church was unequivocal: trading and owning humans was a sin that put you in danger of eternal damnation. These African men and women were bearers of the divine image, just like every other human, and as such, the only proper way to treat them was with love. To treat them as property was an affront to God, and the pronouncements coming from the Vatican made this clear as soon as it becomes an issue.

For example, in 1435, at the beginning of the age of exploration and colonization, Pope Eugene IV issued a papal bull, *Sicut Dudum*, excoriating "some Christians" for committing "illicit and evil deeds" against the native people of the Canary Islands, including subjecting them to "perpetual slavery" and selling them "to other persons." Eugene demanded that all the enslaved natives of the Canary Islands be freed within fifteen days, or their captors would be excommunicated. More than fifty years before Columbus set sail, the Church had prohibited enslaving native peoples.

A series of papal pronouncements reiterating this position followed. As Catholic historian Steve Weidenkopf explains,

In 1537, Pope Paul III (r. 1534–1549) issued a bull, *Sublimus Dei*, which taught that native peoples were not to be enslaved. In 1591, Gregory XIV (r. 1590–1591) promulgated *Cum Sicuti,* which was addressed to the bishop of Manila in the Philippines and reiterated his predecessors' prohibitions against enslaving native peoples. In the seventeenth century, Urban VIII (r. 1623–1644) promulgated *Commissum Nobis* (1639) in support of the Spanish king's (Philip IV) edict prohibiting enslavement of the Indians in the New World.[28]

As the African slave trade developed, subsequent popes condemned slavery as well. In 1741, for example, Benedict

XIV (r. 1740–1758) issued *Immensa Pastorum*, which reiterated that the penalty for enslaving Indians was excommunication. Weidenkopf goes on to note that "papal denunciations of slavery were so harsh and so frequent that the colonial Spanish instituted a law forbidding the publication of papal documents in the colonies without prior royal approval."

Searching for Justification

The Protestants in New England didn't care what the Catholic Church taught, so they didn't worry about pronouncements from the pope. Scripture was their only guide, so to the Bible they turned for guidance. Or, more accurately, to the Bible they turned for justification. Slavery was making them money, after all (more on the almighty dollar in the next chapter), and so it would be helpful if the Bible would support it.

Some colonists tried to accomplish this by arguing that Africans were savage animals that were not fully human and therefore had no souls.[29] That being the case, the colonists argued, Scripture's clear demands for Christian charity didn't apply to them. When Jesus said "whatever you wish that men would do to you, do so to them" (Matt. 7:12), he wasn't referring to Africans, these people reasoned, because Africans weren't people. They didn't rise to the status of "others."

In using this approach, the Christian colonists were like the religious leader to whom Jesus told the parable of the Good Samaritan. In trying to free himself from the command to "love your neighbor as yourself," the expert in the law asks Jesus, "Who is my neighbor?"—clearly insinuating that some, such as Samaritans, don't fall into that category and therefore don't need to be loved.

The Curse of Ham

Some colonists realized this and accepted that the Africans were fellow human beings. However, that doesn't mean they wanted to stop slavery. They simply needed a different biblical justification to keep the practice going. Many found it in the book of Genesis.

According to Khaldun, one theory that had already been in circulation for many years by his time was derived from Genesis 9:18–29. In that passage of Scripture, Noah gets drunk, and his son Ham commits some kind of transgression against him. As a consequence, Noah curses Ham's son, Canaan. The exact nature of Ham's sin has long been debated, as has the interpretation of the curse. During the time of the slave trade, though, many Protestant preachers taught that "Negroes were the children of Ham the son of Noah, and that they were singled out to be black as the result of Noah's curse, which produced Ham's color and the slavery God inflicted upon his descendants."[30] In a 1615 address to Virginia planters, the Reverend Thomas Cooper said that white Shem, one of Noah's good sons, "shall be Lord over" the "cursed race of Cham" (Noah's son Ham) in Africa. In 1625, clergyman Samuel Purchas published four volumes of travel manuscripts, which referred to Africans as "filthy sodomits, sleepers, ignorant, beast, disciples of Cham . . . to whom blacke darknesse is reserved for ever."[31]

The "Curse of Ham" passage would go on to have a long and ignominious history in the annals of American racism, and we will return to it later in this chapter for closer examination. For now, I'll point out that Protestant slavery supporters quickly grabbed onto this passage to justify their actions in a way that was simply not available to Catholics. Again, that's not to say that Catholics weren't participating in the slave trade, but rather that if a Catholic happened to privately accept the racist "Curse of Ham" interpretation of Scripture in defense of slavery, he was openly defying the teachings of the Church by doing so. Within the Bible Alone framework, Protestants could twist the Genesis 3 passage without any outside authoritative accountability.

Servants and Masters

This Scripture-twisting worked for some colonists, but not everyone was convinced. Puritan minister Cotton Mather, for example, saw Africans as fully human and even in need of the gospel.[32] Based on his reading of the Bible, he chastised slave owners for neglecting the spiritual welfare of their slaves: "How canst thou love thy Negro, and be willing to see him ly under the rage of sin, and the wrath of God?"[33] To help remedy the situation, Mather started a "Society of Negroes" on Sunday evenings in hopes of evangelizing the Africans. In another example, Anglican Thomas Bray helped found the Society for the Propagation of the Gospel in Foreign Parts (SPG) to help spread the gospel to non-Europeans.

These efforts didn't go over very well with the white congregants, who worried that freedom from the wages of sin would lead to freedom from slavery. (According to English tradition, one was not to make slaves of fellow Christians.) Unfortunately, Mather and other Christians leaders worked diligently to dispel that concern, assuring slaveholders that the Bible did not grant liberty to Christian slaves.

One popular argument, for example, found "biblical" support for slavery in passages that speak of submission to authority. Ephesians 6:5 was a favorite: "Slaves, obey your earthly masters with fear and trembling." In his widely read 1618 tome "An Entire Commentary on the Whole of

Ephesians," Puritan Paul Baynes expanded on this passage by explaining that some servants, such as the "blackamores with us" are "perpetually put under the power of the master," because they are more "slavish." He notes that these types of servants are partly in their state of subjection due to "the curse of God for sin" and that they sometimes have to be forced into captivity to fulfill their appointed state.[34]

Indeed, some argued, being forced into slavery was good for the slaves in that it allowed them to be introduced to the gospel. "Who can tell," wrote Mather, "but that God may have sent this poor creature into my hands, that so one of the elect may by my means be called, and by my instruction be made wise unto salvation!"[35] Others added that becoming a Christian would help a slave grow in the virtues of humility, hard work, and obedience, which would make him a better slave for his master.

"Scriptural" Dualism

Mather's theology was built on his belief in a sharp, practically gnostic dualism between body and soul, as well as between this world and the next. For Mather and many of his Protestant brethren, the only thing that really mattered was the soul getting to heaven. Worldly, bodily existence just wasn't worth worrying about, especially when applied to slaves. In a talk titled "The Negro Christianized," he preached: "The state of your Negroes in this world, must be low, and mean, and abject—a state of servitude. No great things in this world can be done for them. Something, then, let there be done toward their welfare in the world to come. . . . The blood of the souls of your poor Negroes lies upon you, and the guilt of their barbarous impieties, and superstitions, and their neglect of God and their souls, if you are willing to do nothing toward the salvation of their souls." In the next line, Mather explains that he is basing his direction on Jeremiah 2:34: "In thy skirts is found the blood of souls."[36]

With all of this "biblical" evidence, Mather and others convinced slaveholders that they could save slaves' souls but still leave their bodies in bondage. To ensure slaveholders even more that evangelism wouldn't lead to freedom, one SPG missionary even created baptismal vows that included a promise before God that the slave did not seek the sacrament out of a desire for freedom "from the duty and obedience you owe your master."[37]

Evangelizers also successfully pushed colonial governments to declare that slaves would remain the property of their masters even after baptism, and they asked Britain to issue a formal statement confirming the same, which Britain did. As a result, evangelizing could continue without the "threat" that this would end slavery. The Virginia General Assembly even encouraged "white enslavers to evangelize their human chattel since baptized slaves would not be freed." In the words of the assembly,

> Masters, freed from this doubt, may more carefully endeavor the propagation of Christianity by permitting children, though slaves, or those of greater growth if capable, to be admitted to that sacrament."[38]

The Biblical Road to Civil War

The relationship between early American biblical justifications for slavery and the lengths to which southern Christians later went to defend it cannot be overstated. In colonial America, Protestant defenders of slavery, *using Scripture as their authority*, gave the institution a divine stamp of approval, a move that would resonate for centuries. As professors Michael Emerson and Christian Smith point out:

> In an effort to garner support for Christianizing activities, the clergy not only reaffirmed the appropriateness of slavery as an institution, but gave it cosmic status, solidifying its position in America. Moreover, they unintentionally laid the groundwork for the more advanced nineteenth-century pro-slavery biblically-based doctrines. As theologian Ernst Troeltsch concluded, the "teachings and practice of the church constituted one of the main sanctions for [slavery's] perpetuation."[39]

In other words, the Protestant Christianity practiced in colonial America not only perpetuated slavery, but made it harder to root out of American culture precisely because those who supported it were convinced that God was on their side. This phenomenon was made possible by *sola scriptura*, and it only got worse in the nineteenth century, when abolitionist movements started to grow worldwide. In response, supporters of slavery became even more stridently biblical and theological in their defense. With no outside interpretive authority to undermine them, their racist interpretations gained a wide following.

Some interpreters went to the Old Testament for support. For example, Presbyterian pastor George D. Armstrong published "The Christian Doctrine of Slavery," in which he justified American racism by appealing to the biblical sin of Ham. Armstrong continued the tradition, which we examined earlier, of arguing that Ham's descendants were Africans, and as such, all Africans were meant for perpetual enslavement.[40]

Armstrong and others pointed out several other biblical passages to support slavery. They noted that Abraham and all the patriarchs held slaves (Gen. 21:9–10) and that the Ten Commandments mentioned slavery twice, showing God's implicit acceptance of it (Exod. 20:10, 17).[41]

The New Testament also bolstered the slaveholder's case, in Armstrong's opinion. After all, the apostle Paul returned the runaway slave, Philemon, to his master (Phil. 12) and commanded slaves to obey those who "owned" them (Eph. 6:5–8). Also, the Roman world had slavery, and Jesus never spoke against it—not to mention that everyone is to obey the governing authorities (Rom. 13:1, 7).[42]

These passages and more provided the backdrop for immensely wide Christian support of slavery. Biblical and theological pronouncements about God's support for slavery came from all quarters. For example, the Presbyterian Church in the Confederate States of America talked about the "divine appointment of domestic servitude" and states that its members "hesitate not to affirm that it is the peculiar mission of the Southern Church to conserve the institution of slavery, and to make it a blessing both to master and slave."[43]

As the battle with the abolitionists heated up, Christian supporters of slavery began to see their mission not only as keeping their cultural institution alive, but defending Scripture. Presbyterian Henry Van Dyke went so far as to claim that those who questioned his position were guilty of sacrilege: "When the abolitionist tells me that slaveholding is sin, in the simplicity of my faith in the Holy Scriptures, I point him to this sacred record, and tell him, in all candor, as my text does, that his teaching blasphemes the name of God and his doctrine."[44]

Van Dyke was not alone in this approach. Indeed, the idea that abolitionists were fighting the Bible, Christianity, and ultimately God himself became widespread in the

South. It did not matter that the abolitionists were using the same Bible that the slaveholders were in order to call for an end to slavery. It did not matter that, on the surface, the abolitionist message that all men are created in the image of God and worthy of love, and that we must apply Jesus' Golden Rule to everyone, including Africans, seemed biblical. From a slaveholder's perspective, the abolitionists were false Christians who were interpreting the Bible incorrectly.

Just as in Reformation debates over doctrine, all sides claimed the mantle of true Christianity and labeled their opponents enemies of God. For example, Southern Methodist minister J. W. Tucker told a Confederate audience in 1862, "Your cause is the cause of God, the cause of Christ, of humanity. It is a conflict of truth with error—of Bible with Northern infidelity—of pure Christianity with Northern fanaticism."[45] On the other side, Episcopalian Bishop Thomas March of Rhode Island told a Northern militia, "It is a holy and righteous cause in which you enlist . . . God is with us . . . the Lord of Hosts is on our side."[46]

It is no surprise, then, that many American denominations split over the issue of slavery. Today the Southern Baptist Convention is the nation's largest Protestant group, but the only reason we have a "Southern" Baptist Convention is that in 1845 they split from the Northern Baptists over slavery. The same thing happened with the Methodist Episcopal Church and the Presbyterians. The newly formed "Southern Presbyterian Church" issued a resolution in 1864 stating, "We hesitate not to affirm that it is the peculiar mission of the Southern Church to conserve the institution of slavery, and to make it a blessing to master and slave." They went on to decree that the Northern dogma that slavery was inherently sinful was "unscriptural and fanatical . . . one of the most pernicious heresies of modern times."[47]

This is where *sola scriptura* had brought America. In his masterful work, *The Civil War as a Theological Crisis*, Protestant historian Mark Noll summarizes the situation well:

> The political standoff that led to war was matched by an interpretive standoff. No common meaning could be discovered in the Bible, which almost everyone in the United States professed to honor and which was, without a rival, the most widely read text of any kind in the whole country.[48]

Noll is not the only historian to point out that the "interpretive standoff" helped lead the country to the Civil War. The fact that both supporters and opponents of slavery saw their fight as a religious crusade to save true Christianity certainly helped fuel the motivation for war. Paul Johnson notes that "to judge by the many hundreds of sermons and special prayers which have survived, ministers were among the most fanatical on both sides." He concludes, "The churches played a major role in the dividing of the nation, and it is probably true that it was the splits in the churches which made a final split of the nation inevitable."[49]

More than Just Slavery

Ultimately, the battle over whether or not Scripture condoned slavery was never really about slavery. It was about money, power, and racism.

Even when the war ended and slavery was outlawed, Protestant racism remained as strong as ever.

For example, let us consider Benjamin M. Palmer, pastor of the First Presbyterian Church in New Orleans. His 1960 "Thanksgiving Sermon" was published widely throughout the South and did perhaps more than other public utterances of the time to bring Louisiana to the side of secession. In it he explains that as followers of Jesus Christ, his listeners are duty-bound to God, their slaves (the "most helpless" race under the sun), and the "civilized world" to defend the institution of slavery against the "atheistic" North. He then invokes Genesis 13:5–13, the story in which the herdsmen of Abraham and Lot get into a quarrel and separate, to argue that the South just may need to do the same.[50]

After the war, Palmer did not change his attitude. He simply switched slavery for segregation, again basing his argument on the supposed inferiority of the black race.[51] He stated that African Americans "have never been stimulated to become a self-supporting people, under well-regulated institutions and laws" and that they tend to fall back into "their original state of degradation and imbecility."[52] As such, during Reconstruction, when the Louisiana state legislature attempted to integrate New Orleans public schools, Palmer's church led the movement to create a private educational system that would admit only white students.[53]

The "Biblical" Foundation of a Segregated Society

Unfortunately, Palmer's was not the first, or the only, Protestant community to support segregation. In fact, these communities had long been drivers of it.[54] Where in Scripture did they find their justification to keep black and white separate? In a later address to the Synod of Mississippi of the Presbyterian Church titled "A Christian View of Segregation," G.T. Gillespie offered an overview of several passages commonly used to support the separation of the races. They included the separation of Cain from the other branch of the human family (Gen. 4:11–26), the negative consequences of intermarriage (Gen. 6:1–7), the division of Noah's family after the flood

(Gen. 9:18–29), the origin of linguistic differences at the tower of Babel (Gen. 11:19), the call of Abraham to a separated life (Gen. 12–25), the warnings of Moses against intermarriage with other peoples (Deut. 7:3), Ezra's condemnation of mixed marriages (Ezra 9–10), the fact that Jesus accepted racial distinctions and sent the apostles only to the house of Israel on their first mission (Matt. 10:5–6), and Paul's acceptance of his identity as a member of the Jewish race.[55]

Segregation of the churches lent moral justification to segregation in other areas of life, and "Jim Crow laws" designating "white only" train cars, buses, restaurants, and other public places became commonplace. Indeed, without Christians supporting them, these laws might never have existed. In all of this, the southern Christians still firmly believed they were being true to Scripture, and *sola scriptura* proved entirely inadequate to teach them otherwise or to reign in the evils that their racism subsequently produced.

Indeed, even throughout the sixties into the seventies, Evangelicals supported their prejudice with the same "scriptural" arguments that had been used since before the Civil War. For example, in 1965, Clifford E. McLain published *The Place of Race*, in which he made a "biblical case" for segregation by pointing to the sin of Noah's son Ham.[56] At the same time, Baptist pastor Carey Daniel preached a sermon called "God, the Original Segregationist," in which he too harkened back to Genesis to argue that Ham's descendants, by which he meant people of African descent, were responsible for God's judgment on Sodom and Gomorrah. Further, he wrote, "the Bible clearly implies that the Negroes' black skin is the result of Ham's immorality at the time of his father Noah's drunkenness. For example, in Jeremiah 13:23 we read, 'Can the Ethiopian change his skin, or the leopard his spots? Then may ye also do good, that are accustomed to do evil.' Here the black skin of the Negro is obviously a symbol of evil."[57]

In 1960, Bob Jones Sr., the founder of the university that bears his name, preached what he considered one of his "most important" radio sermons ever: "Is Segregation Scriptural?" In it he argued that the Bible is absolutely clear that races should remain completely separate, even though "some people are dumb" and have put "their own opinion above the Word of God" because they have been influenced by a "Satanic effort to undermine people's faith in the Bible." As his main text, Jones went to Acts 17:26: "[God] hath made of one blood all nations of men for to dwell on the face of the earth and hath determined the times before appointed, and the bounds of their habitation." According to Jones, "That says that God Almighty fixed the bounds of their habitation. That is as clear as anything that was ever said," meaning that God wants the races to be separated.[58]

This provides a good example of how "biblically supported" racism adapted to the post–Civil War years and even the post–civil rights years. The laws continued to change, but racism remained.

Indeed, Bob Jones fought the law for decades. Even in the face of *Brown v. Board of Education* and the Civil Rights Act, his university remained a whites-only school until the early 1970s, when it finally allowed married black students to enroll. Then, even after allowing single black students in 1975, Bob Jones University prohibited interracial dating, a ban that was kept in place until the year 2000![59]

The Klan

The Ku Klux Klan first rose to prominence following the Civil War as a vigilante group dedicated to white supremacy.

It then reappeared in force in 1915, when Methodist preacher William Joseph Simmons climbed Stone Mountain in Georgia, built an altar, set fire to a cross, and announced the Klan's revival. Beneath the altar, they laid a U.S. flag, a sword, and a Bible.[60]

The twentieth-century version of the Klan was as an explicitly white Protestant group, organized specifically to fight not only the ongoing presence of free blacks, but Catholic and Jewish immigration from Europe as well. *Klankraft* made heavy use of the cross and the Bible in its ceremonies and literature and claimed to be cleansing the country of undesirables out of "sublime reverence for our Lord and Savior."[61] Their primary symbol, the MIOAK (which stands for "Mystic Insignia of a Klansman") or the *blood drop cross*, features a white cross with a red teardrop at the center, symbolizing the atonement and sacrifice of Jesus, as well as others who have shed their blood for the white race.

The KKK can be understood only in light of its Protestant religious identity, writes Kelly Baker in *The Gospel According to the Klan: The KKK's Appeal to Protestant America*. She notes that Hiram Wesley Evans, the second imperial wizard of the Klan, saw its founding as a second Reformation.

Evans believed that the Klan had the potential to reform Christianity much in the same way that Martin Luther had "saved" the church within the first Reformation. The church was no longer able to lead such a movement because of fractious denominationalism, but the Klan, based on the Bible, with God and Jesus as its "soul," could bring about "universal and rock-bottom reform." The Klan crafted its own form of Protestantism, which highlighted dissent (protest), individualism, militancy, and a strong commitment to the works of Jesus.[62]

That focus on Jesus came with "biblical" support. KKK teachings went to the Gospels to support their view of Jesus as the original Klansman, touting his supposed anti-Catholicism by noting his disobedience to the high priests and claiming that he taught his followers to worship their heavenly father in the way their consciences best saw fit. The Klan's national publication, the *Kourier*, wrote against "insidious priestcraft" and argued that "to break the people of his day from such enslavement, Jesus boldly declared: 'Ye shall know the truth, and the truth shall make you free'"[63] (John 8:32).

The Klan also taught that Jesus was concerned with maintaining racial purity. Noting that he came to the Jews first (see Matt. 15:24), they argued that this was proof that his allegiance was to "his own race, blood, and religion." Other Klan preachers went to St. Paul's writing for support for their insidious agenda. Reverend W.C. Wright preached a sermon (which was also circulated as a pamphlet) titled "The Twelfth Chapter of Romans as a Klansman's Law of Life" in which he interpreted Paul's opening line, "I beseech you therefore, brethren," as "reminder that we are brethren not only in a common cause, but by racial blood as well."[64]

This message had massive appeal in early twentieth-century America. It is important to realize that the Klan was not a fringe movement at the margins of society; it attracted millions of Protestant members all over the country, from New York to Oregon and California. Indeed, it was stronger in the north than in the south.[65] *The Birth of a Nation*, a 1915 film celebrating the Klan's founding, was a monster hit and became one of the first movies ever shown in the White House.

Protestants informed by *sola scriptura* even gave moral sanction even to one of the Klan's favorite methods of racist terror—the brutal and widely tolerated practice of lynching. Two-time governor and U.S. senator from South Carolina Cole Blease described the ability "of the Caucasian race to dispose of the offending blackamore without the benefit of a jury" as a "divine right."[66] And as Protestant theologian Reinhold Niebuhr observed, "If there were a drunken orgy somewhere, I would bet ten to one a church member was not in it . . . but if there were a lynching, I would bet ten to one a church member was in it."[67]

Christian Silence and Moderation

"Biblically supported" racism continued to be a problem through the civil rights era of the 1950s and 1960s. Not every Christian during that era supported racist policies. However, for the most part, even those that didn't actively work to segregate and discriminate didn't speak up or do much else to oppose it.

To support this position biblically, Protestants such as Billy Graham (at least early in his career) fell back on the same type of dualistic defense that had been used to justify saving slaves' souls while leaving their bodies in chains. Graham argued that he was interested in getting people's souls to heaven, not changing their situation here on earth. For example, after a meeting in Mississippi where he was criticized by both sides of the issue for holding a rally that was open to all races, but was segregated, he told reporters, "I feel that I have been misinterpreted on racial segregation. We follow the existing social customs in whatever part of the country in which we minister. As far as I have been able to find in my study of the Bible, it has nothing to say about segregation or non-segregation. I came to Jackson to preach only the Bible and not to enter into local issues."[68]

This position was buttressed by Graham's reading of the book of Revelation: that the world would not get better until the return of Jesus at the end of the age. After Martin Luther

King Jr.'s[69] "I Have a Dream" speech, for example, Graham dismissed King's assertion that protests could create a community where "down in Alabama little black boys and little black girls will join hands with little white boys and white girls."[70] According to Graham, "only when Christ comes again will the little white children of Alabama walk hand in hand with little black children."[71] As such, the most prudent course of action, believed Graham at the time, was to listen to the words of Romans 13 and "submit to governing authorities, for there is no authority except that which God has established" (v. 1). Speaking to the volatile civil rights situation in Alabama, Graham said, "Only a spiritual and moral awakening" could solve the problem. In the meantime, all parties should obey the laws, "no matter how much we may dislike them. If the law says that I cannot march or I cannot demonstrate, I ought not to march and I ought not to demonstrate. And if the law tells me that I should send my children to a school where there are both races, I should obey that law also. Only by maintaining law and order are we going to keep our democracy and our nation great."[72]

The fact that one of the most influential and acclaimed Protestant leaders of his age could use his own interpretation of a verse in the Bible, absent any governing authority, to justify following obviously cruel and inhumane laws—indeed, the logic here goes, to follow *any* law, *no matter how* cruel and inhumane, just because the government decreed it—shows again the futility of building a solid moral foundation upon *sola scriptura*.

Two Common Objections

Before moving on, let's answer an objection I always get: "What about all the good that Bible-believing Protestant evangelicals have done for civil rights, and all the bad that Catholics have done?"

First, let's affirm that Protestants have accomplished great work for justice. Indeed, I've already talked about one: Martin Luther King Jr. As we noted earlier, of course Protestants can be holy people whose private reading of Scripture can motivate them to do many good things for God and man, and history is full of examples of such people. Certainly, the abolitionist movement in America was driven by righteous indignation fueled in part by the Bible. But I think this underscores rather than refutes the critique of *sola scriptura*. Without an infallible authority to interpret Scripture within an authoritative tradition, Bible reading produced both abolitionists and slavers; appeals to Scripture justified both racist segregation and the call to universal brotherhood.

And let's affirm that individual Catholics have been on the wrong side of this battle throughout history as well. For example, Augustus Tolton was the first black man born in America to become a priest, but the former slave had to travel to Rome to be trained because no American seminary would admit him. During the civil rights era, Catholics could be found fighting against integration alongside racist Protestants. During the mid-century battles over housing policy, certain priests led campaigns to uphold segregation, including one in Buffalo, New York, who tried to deny public housing for African American war workers.[73]

THE CATHOLIC DIFFERENCE

So Catholics may be sinners, too, but the Catholic Church is different, and the history of Catholicism in America illustrates its contrast with Protestantism on this issue.

For example, during the Civil War era, America was deeply divided, and Catholics fought on both sides of the war. (The Church did not take an official political stance in favor of either the North or South.) However, in the midst of the division, Catholics displayed a profound and unique moral and spiritual unity that their Protestant friends and neighbors couldn't match. By the end of the war, according to historian George Marlin, "the Church's prestige was greatly enhanced. She had remained unified; her soldiers had fought bravely, and Americans had witnessed uncountable acts of Catholic charity."[74] Civil War scholar Mark Summers offers this poignant snapshot and analysis:

> Along with the thousands of soldiers that fought in the ranks were hundreds of priests who ministered to the troops and Catholic Sisters who assisted as nurses and sanitary workers. Catholic soldiers were at a religious disadvantage compared to the Protestant comrades, as the Church lacked enough priests to both serve in the army and minister to the congregations at home. Nevertheless, Catholic priests heard confession, comforted the men, and celebrated Mass prior to battle. More than eight different orders of nuns served the soldiers during the war. Before the organization of the American Red Cross, nuns were among the most organized and experienced nurses available to serve the army. Catholic sisters were praised for their assistance to all soldiers, North and South, Catholic or Protestant. When observing this ministry, a Protestant doctor remarked to a Catholic bishop that "there must be some wonderful unity in Catholicity which nothing can destroy, not even the passions of war."
>
> Indeed, it was this unity of the Catholic Church which proved unique among American Christianity. While

Protestant denominations split over theological and sectional lines, the Catholic Church stood as the only major church which remained united during the war, even if its congregants fought on opposite sides. While the Civil War brought violence and destruction to the nation on a horrific scale, it did provide the Catholic Church in America, and its largely immigrant community, a means to show the "better angels of our nature" and the loyalty and Christian sense of duty of its parishioners; a service and devotion which continues to the present day.[75]

One reason for this continued unity is that the Catholic Church has the theological and philosophical basis needed to provide a unified teaching, and it has done so with regard to racism and slavery. We've already discussed several papal bulls and pronouncements condemning racism and the slave trade during the initial exploration of the New World, and these persisted throughout the eighteenth and nineteenth centuries. Pope Gregory XVI's 1839 bull *In Supremo*, for instance, reiterated papal opposition to slavery and forbade any clergyman or layperson from presuming to defend as permissible this horrific practice, no matter what excuse or pretext he might present. In 1888 and again in 1890, Pope Leo XIII forcefully condemned slavery and sought its elimination where it persisted in parts of South America and Africa.

Now, it is true that not all American clergy gave vocal support to the papal pronouncements, and this opened the Church up to critiques of just how strongly it opposed slavery.[76] However, the fact remains that the authoritative teaching was clear.

Also, even though it is not always implemented well, the Catholic Church has the theological foundation and authoritative structure to effectively deal with clergy and congregants who are disobeying the teachings of the Church (in other words, sinning against God). Protestantism, as we have seen, simply has no such foundation or structure. When a Catholic dissents from Church teaching (such as publicly being pro-abortion or blatantly racist) or lives in open disobedience to the Church, the Church has a way to keep that person accountable. For example, it can censure him, remove his priestly faculties, and even excommunicate him. Even if the authorities of the Catholic Church hierarchy don't always operate within this structure and use their authority properly, the Catholic Church nonetheless has a system in place that makes confronting sin possible in a way that *sola scriptura* lacks.

On top of that, the Church's structure provides no way to justify a sinful position. An individual Catholic can't reasonably say, "God told me the Catholic Church was wrong on this." To do so is to cease to be Catholic, either practically or formally.[77]

The story of Archbishop Joseph Rummel of New Orleans offers a good case study in what Catholicism can do that Protestantism cannot. After becoming archbishop in 1935, he became well known as a champion of the poor and oppressed, leading a relief program for refugees fleeing the Nazis in World War II and fighting for racial justice and desegregation. During his time in New Orleans, he also fought for full integration of parishes and Catholic schools. He removed "white" and "colored" signs from the archdiocese and ordered that "no further discrimination or segregation" take place "in the pews, at the Communion rail, at the confessional, and in parish meetings." He later closed a church that refused to welcome a black priest, chastising parishioners for their "act of injustice, uncharitableness, and irreverence."[78]

His battle with the segregationists was just beginning. As the archdiocese prepared to fully integrate its schools, it

faced opposition from powerful leaders such as state senator E.W. Gravolet, who threatened to cut off state support
to Catholic schools. In response, the archbishop sent out
letters to the most vocal opponents of segregation, warning them that if they didn't comply with Church teaching,
they would be excommunicated. This means they would
be barred from receiving the Eucharist and the other sacraments, along with other honors due to the faithful, such as
a Catholic burial. Essentially, they were being cut off from
the source of eternal life.

The warning was heeded, and most of those who were
fighting the Church ceased their activities. However, three
leaders did not, and on April 16, 1962, Rummel excommunicated Leander Perez; Jackson G. Ricau, secretary of
Citizens Council of South Louisiana; and Mrs. B.J. Gaillot
Jr., president of Save Our Nation, Inc., for continuing "to
hinder his orders or provoke the devoted people of this ven-
erable archdiocese to disobedience or rebellion in the matter
of opening our schools to all Catholic children."[79]

This move won the battle. According to reports, "most
Catholics in the area seemed to lend little support to Perez,
Gaillot and Ricau while the excommunicants seemed stun-
ned by the action."[80] Ricau and Perez were later reinstated
into the Church after public shows of repentance, and the
schools became fully integrated without violence or a drop
in registration.

Ecclesial authority was used effectively in other regions as
well. A Maryland delegation told Cardinal Patrick O'Boyle
that it would take ten years for their parishes to be ready for
desegregation. "Well, gentleman," said the cardinal, "we're
going to do it tomorrow."[81] In another example, an angry
group of 700 white parents threatened to take Archbishop
Joseph Ritter to court after he ordered the integration of

Catholic schools in St. Louis in 1947. The archbishop refused to meet with their leaders and instead had a letter read in Mass that Sunday threatening to excommunicate any participants in the suit. This quickly changed the mind of John P. Barrett, chairman of the new Catholic Parents Association. "I don't want to do anything that would jeopardize my religion," he said. Two weeks later, opposition collapsed as Barrett voted to disband the group.[82]

Toothless Religion

Within the Protestant framework of *sola scriptura*, this type of moral authority isn't possible. That's not to say Protestants haven't tried, but it simply doesn't work. As we discussed earlier, if the Bible is the sole authority for faith and morals, then each individual is ultimately the arbiter of his own standard. Each person interprets the Bible in the way he wants. Protestant ecclesial communities and denominations, then, are essentially voluntary associations of people who interpret the Bible in the same way, or at least a similar enough way that they can all get along.[83]

Historically in America, to "become a member" of a local congregation, you had to sign off on a "statement of faith" that listed the doctrines to which this local group adhered. Similarly, there might have been a "code of conduct" in place, telling you what is and is not accepted. These are fairly uncommon now, as cheap cars and good roads have made it easier for people to travel to a church they like. That leads to the problem with Protestant ecclesial communities' structure and discipline: they don't work because they can't work under *sola scriptura*. Think about it: what happens to a Protestant believer who disagrees with the doctrine or doesn't live according to the standard of a particular community? He doesn't go to that community! It's as simple as that. He either makes his own community or finds a new one. How can the leaders of a community exercise authority and discipline on people who don't recognize any authority above themselves and their Bible and can easily find somewhere else to go where they will be accepted? They can't. Therefore, they don't. *Sola scriptura* took the moral teeth out of religion, and Protestant culture has paid the price ever since.

In the next chapter, we will see how this applies to a very modern sin afflicting America and the developed world.

CHAPTER 3

BLE$$ED

Kim[84] had no idea the numbers were so high. 177 orders in the previous twelve months. 1,427 total items purchased since starting her Amazon account eight years ago. $40,981.60 paid. And, in what she says might be "the saddest part of the story," she doesn't have a clue where any of those purchases are, "or even where they might be."[85]

Kim is hardly unique. In an article about "doom shopping" during the 2020 coronavirus pandemic, columnist Whizy Kim talked to women all over the country about their shopping habits. They each described compulsively buying items that they absolutely didn't need, just to help them feel better. A woman named Victoria described spending over $200 a month on "stupid things"—such as four bathing suits, even though she lives a thousand miles from the nearest beach. Hanna spent about $320 a month on clothes, not because she needed them—she wasn't going to the office or anywhere else—but simply because "the prices are too good to pass up." Melissa spent between $500 and $1,000 a month online (she was too scared to look and find out exactly), purchasing more than ten Halloween costumes . . . for her Corgi.[86] And Samantha spent about $500 monthly on what she called "non-essentials," going so far as to admit that the thought of not buying something she wants gave her anxiety.

Buy, Use, Discard, Repeat

These women are not outliers. Compulsive shopping is becoming so pervasive and problematic that psychotherapists are developing new categories of mental health conditions to address it.[87] (One of the fastest-growing trends in retail is buying items from your phone in the middle of the night![88]) But we don't need a psychological classification in place to recognize that most Americans buy more stuff than they need. Even those of us who aren't getting up in the middle of the night to place orders on Amazon are making time to shop for items that aren't really necessary for day-to-day life. One survey, for example, found that the average American woman has $550 worth of unworn clothing in her closet.[89]

Interestingly, even with all those extra clothes in our closets, Americans are not people that hoard everything. Oh, we do hoard an immense amount of stuff—so much, in fact, that we've made storage unit companies one of the most solid investments of the twenty-first century[90]—but we also get rid of a lot. Eventually, many of those closets get purged. The Council for Textile Recycling estimates that the average American throws away about seventy pounds of clothes each year,[91] with 10.5 million tons ending up in landfills.[92] Donation Centers such as Salvation Army and Goodwill struggle to sell even a small fraction of the items they receive.[93]

Our compulsive buying doesn't necessarily mean we are keeping everything we purchase. Rather, shopping is just one part of an ongoing cycle in which we *buy, use, discard,* and then *repeat.* Our addiction to buying clothes (and everything else) is part of the quintessential pastime of the wealthy West: consumerism.

Consumerism and America

Sometime labeled *materialism, commercialism,* or *acquisitiveness,* the never-ending consumeristic cycle of buy, use, discard, and repeat has also been called something else: the "central characteristic of modern life."[94] Americans love to consume. Even in our fractious age, we all seem to agree that it is good to be able to shop and spend. Indeed, it is arguably the strongest unifying theme of American culture. As Brad Gregory notes, "Amid the hyperpluralism of divergent truth claims, meta-physical beliefs, moral values, and life priorities, ubiquitous practices of consumerism are more than anything else the cultural glue that holds Western societies together."[95] We may disagree on any number of political and social issues, but we all value the chance to get 70 percent off on Black Friday.

Indeed, we celebrate shopping as one of our most treasured activities. (Black Friday and Cyber Monday are now at least on par with Thanksgiving.) In that sense, consumerism has a strong ethical, and even quasi-religious, quality to it. Americans take as given that it is morally good to be a consumer. To put that more formally, we believe the following creed: *It is good to buy whatever we want, whenever we want, in as large of a quantity as we want.*

This belief system is so deeply entrenched in the American psyche that it has affected even that way we talk about freedom. Today, to be "free" always includes the freedom to practice consumerism. Think of the patriotic appeals to keep shopping and going to movies after the 9-11 attacks. "If you don't keep spending money on stuff that isn't necessary, the terrorists will have won." The *New York Times* expressed a similar sentiment in an opinion piece by Li Yuan in early 2021, arguing that even though pandemic-era governments around the world were greatly restricting freedoms in many areas of life (journalism, religion, even family get-togethers), as long as we have the freedom to buy luxury brand items, we should celebrate.[96]

It's no wonder that young people have now come to define America in consumeristic terms. James Twitchell writes, "Ask any group of teenagers what democracy means to them. You will hear an extraordinary response. Democracy is the right to buy anything you want. Freedom's just another word for lots of things to buy."[97] As Lizabeth Cohen details in her work *A Consumer's Republic*, there has become no essential difference between what it means to be an American and what it means to be a consumer. To be a typical and proper American is, in the words of the fifties-era Ford Motor Company commercial, to have a "constant desire for something newer and better" and to be able to fulfill that desire by getting behind the wheel of a shiny new car.[98]

Of course, it never stops with the new and better car, new and better clothes, or new and better refrigerator. The consumerist life also means getting the new and better TV, new and better house, and new and better everything else. And when the next version comes out, it means doing that all over again.

The Con

Before getting to how this relates to *sola scriptura*, let's take a few moments to address a potential question: is this really that big of a deal? After all, shouldn't we be able to enjoy a few nice things? What exactly is so wrong with consumerism?

Plenty, starting with the fact that it simply doesn't provide the joy that it promises. Consumerism is a giant con, built

RESULTS OF
EAZI
LIVING

on the contradictory message that the key to human happiness is endless acquisition *and* that you should be unhappy with whatever it is you just acquired.[99] The ensuing illogical rat race leads only to despair, as Erik Rittenberry recently described in a viral blog post titled "The American Life is Killing You." He starts the piece this way:

> If you're in the same boat as the typical American, your dilemma might look something like this:
>
> You're enduring some type of chronic illness, overstressed and rushed, unrewarding job, little or no savings, greatly in debt, fat mortgage, two vehicles in the driveway with a five or seven-year loan on each, lots of gadgets and toys to keep you occupied, huge TV, little free time for yourself due to your career and a demanding spouse, weekends filled with . . . senseless entertainment, and a bathroom cabinet heavily stacked with pharmaceutical tic-tacs to help cope with the emptiness of it all.
>
> This is probably you and it's okay. This is considered normal in America. You are a success. You've achieved the American Dream. Your obedience and education and hard work have paid off. Congratulations.
>
> But the problem is that you're miserable and shallow and quite possibly unhealthy and a little dispirited and you'll likely die of either heart disease, cancer, diabetes, Alzheimer's, or suicide in the not-so-distant future—statistically speaking . . . *BRASH PROOF*
>
> This status chasing, security-obsessed, hurried American lifestyle is draining you of your life energy. It's killing you. It has been for some time. And you feel it.
>
> The reason you don't feel alive is because you aren't alive. You're merely going through the motions in a fast-paced, consumer-centered culture that has transformed

our once beautiful land into an asphalt wasteland strewed with digital billboards, fast food joints, soulless malls, and complete carnage.[100]

Ouch. But it only stings because it is true. Consumerism is a dead end, spiritually and physically. And although the religiously agnostic Rittenberry correctly recognizes its failure and goes on to offer some helpful suggestions to counter a consumeristic malaise (get out in nature more, etc.), for a fuller explanation of why consumerism is wrong and dangerous, and what we must do to find true and lasting fulfillment, we go to Scripture and Church tradition.

Idolatry

As Augustine famously wrote in *Confessions*, "Thou hast made us for thyself, O Lord, and our heart is restless until it finds its rest in thee."[101] One reason that consumer items don't satisfy us is in any ultimate sense is that they *can't*; they are created things, and we were made for the Creator.

The meaning of our lives is to live in intimate union with God. As I write in more detail elsewhere,[102] this loving relationship is only possible inasmuch as we value God and everything else according to their proper worth. We must put God first and have no other gods before him (Exod. 20:3). To put anyone or anything above God is to live contrary to reality, and that simply doesn't work. It's like trying to run your gas-powered car on water; it will only lead to the destruction of your car. Trying to operate yourself without God in his proper place will only lead to the destruction of your life.

The biblical term for this disordering of reality is *idolatry*, and Scripture is very clear that idolatry results in catastrophe. As Herbert Schlossberg explains,

The exaltation of possessions to the level of ultimacy is the end of a religious quest, one that seeks and ascribes ultimate meaning. Like all idolatries, it finds ultimate meaning in an aspect of creation rather than in the Creator. And like all idolatries it finds outlet in the destructive pathologies that wreck human lives.[103]

Immorality

How does consumerism wreck lives? One way is by fostering immorality.[104] Those who make their primary focus getting money, and the stuff that money can buy, tend toward unethical behavior and attitudes, either to justify getting more stuff or because their conscience has been deadened due to idolatry. As Paul tells Timothy, "Those who want to get rich fall into temptation and a trap and into many foolish and harmful desires that plunge people into ruin and destruction. For the love of money is a root of all kinds of evil. Some people, eager for money, have wandered from the Faith and pierced themselves with many griefs" (1 Tim. 6:9–10).

Surely that is one reason Jesus warned that it is extremely difficult for a rich man to reach eternal life. When a wealthy man came to Jesus and asked what it takes to attain that prize, Jesus answered, "If you want to be perfect, go, sell your possessions and give to the poor, and you will have treasure in heaven. Then come, follow me" (Matt. 19:21). The man refused and went away sad, at which point Jesus told his disciple, "Truly I tell you, it is hard for someone who is rich to enter the kingdom of heaven. Again I tell you, it is easier for a camel to go through the eye of a needle than for someone who is rich to enter the kingdom of God" (Matt. 19:23).

Here Jesus is simply expanding on the scriptural teaching of which his Jewish listeners should have been well aware:

that prosperity closely accompanies "spiritual complacency, pride, and moral decline."[105] This warning was given clearly in the Pentateuch (Deut. 8:11–14) as well as in the Psalms, which identify the wicked as those who trust in riches rather than in God (Psa. 52:7).

Yet in our culture we tend to think of the materially wealthy as *more* morally upright than the poor. We view those that have a lot of stuff as deserving of those things, as if material possessions were the reward for being virtuous. We make celebrities of rich people, we vote them into office, we devote entire media enterprises to simply watching how they lavishly spend their money. We also entrust large segments of our lives to the authority of rich people, assuming that because they are rich, they know what is best for us. How else to explain taking medical advice from Bill Gates, the software mogul who somehow became a go-to authority on education, agriculture, public health, and other subjects?

All of this is contrary to Scripture and Church tradition. As G.K. Chesterton puts it,

The whole modern world is absolutely based on the assumption, . . . that the rich are trustworthy, which (for a Christian) is not tenable. You will hear. . . that the rich man cannot be bribed. The fact is, of course, that the rich man is bribed; he has been bribed already. That is why he is a rich man. The whole case for Christianity is that a man who is dependent upon the luxuries of this life is a corrupt man, spiritually corrupt, politically corrupt, financially corrupt. There is one thing that Christ and all the Christian saints have said with a sort of savage monotony. They have said simply that to be rich is to be in peculiar danger of moral wreck.[106]

Gluttony

As for the specifics of that moral wreck, let's start with perhaps the most obvious sin associated with consumerism: gluttony. Although generally thought of (if anyone thinks of it at all anymore) in relation to food, gluttony is actually the overconsumption of *anything* to the point of waste, or the consumption of anything that is too luxurious or costly. I'm sure we can all think of examples of individual gluttony in our consumeristic culture, like some in the stories I shared at the beginning of this chapter. However, on a larger scale, one "very remarkable aspect" of this sin, according to Dorothy Sayers, is that it has become the foundation of our entire economic system. Already recognizing this during World War II, she wrote a passage that applies just as well today, and is worth quoting at length:

> Whereas formerly it was considered a virtue to be thrifty and content with one's lot, it is now considered to be the mark of a progressive nation that it is filled with hustling, go-getting citizens, intent on raising their standard of living. And this is not interpreted to mean merely that a decent sufficiency of food, clothes, and shelter is attainable by all citizens. It means much more and much less than this. It means that every citizen is encouraged to consider more, and more complicated, luxuries necessary to his well-being. The gluttonous consumption of manufactured goods had become, before the war, the prime civic virtue . . . this fearful whirligig of industrial finance based on gluttonous consumption, . . . could not be kept up for a single moment without the cooperative gluttony of the consumer . . . the whole system would come crashing down in a day if every consumer were voluntarily to restrict purchases to the things really needed.[107]

Covetousness

Gluttony is closely associated with another deadly sin: *covetousness*. Singled out for its own commandment (Exod. 20:17) and the subject of much attention from Jesus and the New Testament authors (Matt. 7:22, Eph. 5:3–5, Col. 3:5, James 4:2), the greedy desire to have more and more is considered a grievous offense in Scripture and Church tradition. Also known as *avarice*, this sin is compounded when it is accompanied by the neglect of those go without. As Brad Gregory explains, medieval saints such as Francis of Assisi railed against this vice because

> avaricious men and women selfishly sought to augment their superfluous wants at the expense of meeting others' most basic needs. "If brother or sister and naked and lacks daily food, and one of you says to them, 'Go in Peace; keep warm and eat your fill,' and yet you do not supply their bodily needs, what is the good of that? So faith by itself, without works, is dead" (James 2:15–17). The wealthy who neglected the needy sinned not only against justice, as Ambrose and other had maintained, but also against Christianity's central commandment of *caritas*.[108]

For the contemporary Western world, however, not only is covetousness not a sin against justice or *caritas*, it has been, to quote Sayers again, endowed with "glamor on a big scale" and given a new title that it could "carry like a flag":

> It occurred to somebody to call it enterprise. From the moment of that happy inspiration, covetousness has gone forward and never looked back. It has become a swaggering, swash-buckling, piratical sin, going about with its had cocked over its eye, and with pistols tucked into

the tops of its jackboots. Its war cries are "Business Efficiency!" "Free Competition!" "Get Out or Get Under!" and "There's Always Room at the Top!"[109]

In the same way that the "American Dream" has been equated with gluttony, it has become equally defined by avarice. The entire project of striving for whatever we don't currently have is sustained by a constant cultivation of covetousness, primarily through advertising. Digital marketing experts estimate that most Americans are exposed to between 4,000 and 10,000 ads each day,[110] and the implicit message of almost every one is that we should *covet*.

Within this context, America has become a place in which it is very difficult to follow Jesus' teaching against greed. Indeed, it may be more difficult that many of us assume, as Ross Douthat brilliantly explains:

> There's an assumption that Christianity's traditional critique of Mammon worship is aimed primarily at the riches of the rich—the people who are most likely to resemble the camel struggling to nose its way through the needle's eye, as the gospel image has it. But there's a reason that the disciples respond to Jesus' famous simile with a shocked "Who then can be saved?" They understood, as many of today's casual readers might not, that the image implies a broader condemnation of acquisitiveness in all its forms. In Christian teaching, the pursuit of money can be as morally dangerous as the possession of great wealth, and the middle-class striver may be as steeped in sinfulness as an Andrew Carnegie or a Donald Trump. In the story of the camel and the needle's eye, the disciples recognized, all men stand condemned—not because we are all rich, but because almost all of us desire to be so and too often organize our lives around that desire.

That is a hard teaching in any society, but especially in one as steeped in capitalist competition as our own . . . The stringency of Christianity's sexual teachings get most of the press, but the commandment against avarice, if taken seriously, can be the Faith's most difficult by far.[111]

Theft

My daughter works in retail, and the way she tells the story, a woman in her store had so many items stuffed under her clothes that she could barely walk. That didn't keep her from trying to get just one more Michael's item into her pants, though, at which point my daughter called security.

Theft is an acutely rising problem; from cars to clothes to office supplies, more and more merchandise gets stolen each year.[112]

Why? There are likely multiple reasons, of course,[113] but according to Neal Lawson, one of the main drivers of theft is "turbo-consumerism." In an article defending that thesis, Lawson tries to make sense of why a gang of teens mugged his son for his iPod, and starts by pointing out that our whole approach to social identity has changed. There was a time when we were known by what we produced. Our standing in society would have been at least somewhat dependent on what we created. You might have tried to build up a reputation as an excellent welder or shoemaker, while I would have worked hard to become known as a skilled wordsmith. Today, however, "we judge ourselves and each other by what we and they consume . . . It's a world driven by competition for consumer goods and paid-for experiences, of hi-tech and high-end shopping signals that have become the means by which we keep score with each other."[114] It no longer matters what you do or create, it only matters that what you do makes you enough money to flash the latest iPhone and use it to post Instagram pics of your weekend getaway, or at least a social media video of you unboxing your latest Amazon orders.

Lawson also notes that it isn't just what a person *has* that is important, it is also how successful a person is at *getting the new thing.* So, for example, we all understand that teens desire certain brand-name clothes and a particular type of phone, not for the comfort of the clothes or the utility of the device, but for what those brands say about them. However, taking that a step further, in today's "turbo-consumerism," the identity of the teen isn't tied to what phone or jeans he *has now,* but for what new phone or new jeans he is *able to attain,* and how quickly. To be "normal" in today's society, then, is to be able to quickly get the latest new thing—even if, for some, that means stealing it.[115]

Usury

For others, the consumeristic desire to have something quickly, often before they have the ability (or willingness) to actually pay for it, doesn't lead to burglary or robbery but down a different destructive path: high-interest consumer debt.

Americans love to buy things on credit. In 2020, household debt rose to a record 14.3 trillion,[116] with the average Joe making payments not only on big ticket items such as a house, car, and education, but also on small things purchased using credit cards and personal loans. Those with credit card debt owed an average of more than $7,000 in 2020, for a total of 416 billion dollars.[117]

There are many moral aspects to the debt crisis in America, but for our purposes, I want to focus briefly on how our consumeristic easy-credit mindset has opened the door for one particular evil: predatory lending. From payday loans to subprime mortgages aimed at poor communities, charging exorbitant interest rates to those who can least afford it, a practice traditionally known as *usury*, is a huge part of our economy.[118] It is also strongly condemned by Scripture and Church tradition.[119] In the *Inferno*, Dante consigns the merely avaricious, the hoarders, and the spendthrifts, to the fourth circle of Upper Hell. As Nick Baldock comments, "Comparatively, they get off lightly: down in Nether Hell, in the third ring of the Circle of Violence, Dante placed the usurers, along with the blasphemers and the sodomites," because they had done violence to God's creation. "When the machinations of finance were predicated on money earning money, they were predicated on an illusion. It was an attempt to get something for nothing."[120]

Getting something for nothing is now one of the key components of the Western consumeristic system. There are currently more payday lending stores in the U.S. then there are McDonalds restaurants,[121] many charging as much as 600 percent interest on their loans.[122]

Exploitation

We've already talked about how consumerism is idolatry, and how we sabotage our own happiness by placing the pursuit of things over God. One other unfortunate consequence of that pursuit is that we place things over other people as well.

The idea of pursuing consumer items at the expense of other people might conjure up images of a Black Friday shopper elbowing his way through a throng to get to the last big-screen TV, and that certainly fits the point. However, a much bigger problem takes place on a much wider scale, more hidden from sight. I am thinking of the Congolese children who are killed and crippled while mining cobalt to put in our smartphones, laptops, and electric cars.[123] Or the 100,000 Uighur Muslims forced into slave labor factories in Xinjiang, China, spending every day producing everyday items for us, from textiles to tomato paste.[124] Or the workers in Chennai, India, who recently protested outside the Apple distributor they worked for because they hadn't been paid their contracted rate, even after putting up with sweatshop conditions.[125]

Should stories of forced labor, inhuman working conditions, and defrauding of workers bother us during our next trip to the Apple Store or T.J. Maxx? I think they should. God cares deeply about the plight of the poor and gets particularly angry when they are oppressed by the wealthy. "Woe to those who make unjust laws, to those who issue oppressive decrees, to deprive the poor of their rights and withhold justice from the oppressed of my people, making widows their prey and robbing the fatherless. What will you do on the day of reckoning, when disaster comes from afar?" (Isa. 10:1–3). Micah proclaimed God's judgment on those in Judah who "covet fields and seize them, and houses, and take them. They defraud people of their homes, they rob them of their inheritance" (Mic. 2:2). Through the prophet Malachi, God thundered, "Then I will draw near to you for judgment; I will be swift to bear witness against the sorcerers, against the adulterers, against those who swear falsely, against those who oppress the hired workers in their wages, the widow and the orphan, against those who thrust aside the alien, and do not fear me, says the Lord of hosts" (Mal. 3:5).

God is very consistent in placing economic oppression alongside the sins we think about more often, such as adultery and lying, and he promises that judgment is coming on those who persist in these vices. We see this theme throughout the

New Testament as well. For example, James could not be more clear about the danger of the rich oppressing the poor: "Come now, you rich people, weep and wail for the miseries that are coming to you. Your riches have rotted, and your clothes are moth-eaten. Your gold and silver have rusted, and their rust will be evidence against you, and it will eat your flesh like fire. You have laid up treasure for the last days. Listen! The wages of the laborers who mowed your fields, which you kept back by fraud, cry out, and the cries of the harvesters have reached the ears of the Lord of hosts" (James 5:1–4).

That the plan of God revolves around justice for the poor and oppressed can be seen in Jesus' ministry from beginning to end. He announces his mission by quoting from the prophet Isaiah, "The Spirit of the Lord is upon me, because he has anointed me to bring good news to the poor. He has sent me to proclaim release to the captives and recovery of sight to the blind, to let the oppressed go free, to proclaim the year of the Lord's favor." Then, in speaking about the day of judgment, Jesus explains that we will be judged according to how we treat the poor:

> Then the king will say to those at his right hand, "Come, you that are blessed by my Father, inherit the kingdom prepared for you from the foundation of the world; for I was hungry and you gave me food, I was thirsty and you gave me something to drink, I was a stranger and you welcomed me, I was naked and you gave me clothing, I was sick and you took care of me, I was in prison and you visited me." Then the righteous will answer him, "Lord, when was it that we saw you hungry and gave you food, or thirsty and gave you something to drink? And when was it that we saw you a stranger and welcomed you, or naked and gave you clothing? And when was it that we

saw you sick or in prison and visited you?" And the king
will answer them, "Truly I tell you, just as you did it to
one of the least of these who are members of my family,
you did it to me" (Matt. 25: 34–40).

The Catholic Position on Consumerism

Recognizing these truths, the Catholic Church has been
consistent and clear in its condemnation of the sins associated with consumerism. The *Catechism*, for example, expands
on the tenth commandment against coveting by first con-
necting it to theft, robbery, fraud, fornication, and idolatry.
Then is lays down the hammer, as clear as can be, stating
that the commandment

> forbids greed and the desire to amass earthly goods with-
> out limit. It forbids avarice arising from a passion for riches
> and their attendant power. It also forbids the desire to
> commit injustice by harming our neighbor in his temporal
> goods: When the Law says, "You shall not covet," these
> words mean that we should banish our desires for whatever
> does not belong to us. Our thirst for another's goods is im-
> mense, infinite, never quenched. Thus it is written: "He
> who loves money never has money enough" (2536).

In applying this truth, the *Catechism* (quoting the Roman
Catechism of the sixteenth century) recognizes that some will
have a harder time struggling against these "criminal desires,"
people such as "merchants who desire scarcity and rising prices, who cannot bear not to be the only ones buying and selling so that they themselves can sell more dearly and buy more
cheaply" and "those who hope that their peers will be impoverished, in order to realize a profit either by selling to them

or buying from them" (2357). However, these people must remain pure from covetousness, as well as avoid envy, which is "sadness at the sight of another's goods and the immoderate desire to have them for oneself. It is a capital sin" (2359). Popes have also stood strong against the dangers of consumerism. Pope St. John Paul II, for example, wrote in *Sollicitudo Rei Socialis* that the "mere accumulation of goods and services, even for the benefit of the majority, is not enough for the realization of human happiness" and that the "excess availability of every kind of material goods for the benefit of certain social groups, easily makes people slaves of 'possession' and of immediate gratification, with no other horizon than the multiplication or continual replacement of the things already owned with others still better" (28).

That encyclical was promulgated to commemorate Pope St. Paul VI's *Popularum Progressio*, which in turn had built on Pope Leo XIII's classic 1891 social teaching encyclical, *Rerum Noverum*. Both these texts recognized and condemned the immorality and danger of economic injustice.

More recently, Pope Benedict XVI wrote his own encyclical paying tribute to *Popularum Progressio*, titled *Caritas in Veritate,* and he consistently denounced the false idol and "dead-end street" of consumerism.[126] Pope Francis, too, has also been clear in condemning the consumeristic mindset, noting that the "throwaway culture" has extended not just to shopping items we no longer want, but to people as well.[127]

Many Catholics have failed to heed the Church's teachings and warnings against the temptations of consumerism and succumbed to them. Yet this does not make the teaching any less clear or authoritative. As Bishop Oscar Cantu put it, the Church stands "in direct opposition to the reduction of the individual to nothing more than an autonomous rights-bearing consumer."[128]

The Reformation Era

As we have seen, the Catholic Church has been very consistent regarding the evils of mammon. In medieval times, avarice was a deadly sin, wealth for its own sake was dangerous, and usury was immoral. And even as the world became increasingly monetized and consumeristic, the Church held on to its traditional notions.

Unfortunately, then as today, individual Catholics didn't always practice the Church's precepts, and disobedience regarding money matters was widespread among the laity—and worse, among the clergy too. Indeed, in the leadup to the Reformation, this was one of the major criticisms of the hierarchy.

Those who exercised ecclesial authority, safeguarded doctrinal orthodoxy, led the church's worship, and administered its sacraments appeared to many people, clerical as well as lay, as though they were the pioneering, principal violators of the church's own condemnations of avarice—men who, in Tawney's phrase, "preached renunciation and gave a lesson in greed." Most conspicuous among them were the highest ranking members of the clergy—the popes and cardinals at the papal court, along with wealthy bishops in their respective dioceses—who, already long before the Avignonese popes and their courtiers intensified all these trends in the fourteenth century, so often sought to augment their incomes through simony, pluralism, and a deep participation in the economy through the purchase of luxurious material things and the borrowing of large sums of money . . . By the eve of the Reformation, the greediness of the clergy and religious high and low was the most common, longstanding complaint made against them.[129]

However, it is important to note here the nature of that complaint: the problem, as understood by those that were disgusted by this behavior, was that the clergy and religious *were not living up to the moral precepts of the Church to which they belonged.* And, certainly, the critiques included references to Scripture. John Colet, for example, thundered against a gathering of clergy in St. Paul's Cathedral in 1510 by asserting that "every corruption, every ruin of the Church, every scandal of the world comes from the avarice of priests, following Paul's words which again I repeat and impress upon your ears, 'Avarice is the root of all evil!'"[130] He and his hearers, understood that this was not an appeal to Colet's personal interpretation of 1 Timothy 6:10. It was a call to align with the teaching of the Church to which Paul and Timothy belonged, a Church that had received, developed, and presented a clear moral teaching on the evils of greed. Colet's listeners may have ignored the message, but there was no dispute as to the authority on which it was based.

That changed at the Reformation. From Luther's revolution onward, Protestants who wanted to confront sins such as avarice had to appeal to their personal interpretation of Scripture alone. And many did. The history of Protestantism, especially in the earlier years, is full of preachers strongly opposed to greed and acquisitiveness.

Luther himself warned merchants that their desire to maximize profits was "making room for avarice and opening every door and window to hell."[131] He later wrote *On Commerce and Liberty*, in which he reaffirmed the traditional Christian teaching against unjust loans. Other early Protestants such as Martin Buber, Ulrich Zwingli, Jakob Strauss, Thomas Muntzer, and Menno Simons also spoke out against avarice and usury, agreeing with Luther on these topics, even as they disagreed with him vehemently on many others.

But the fact that they had those other disagreements, of course, points to the heart of the problem. Within the *sola scriptura* framework, all doctrinal or moral claims become matters of personal opinion, and therefore are easy to dismiss. As historian George O'Brien explains,

> The Catholic preacher had been the accredited agent of an authority that claimed to be infallible in matters of faith and morals, but the Protestant preacher had no claim to the attention of his audience beyond what he derived from his own education, eloquence, or piety. Moreover, the moral precepts urged by such preachers had none of the compulsory character of the old Catholic ethical code, but were merely invitations to act up to a standard which was approved by the preacher. The value of such preaching depended entirely on the preacher's capacity to convince his listeners, who were at perfect liberty to reject all that he stated, if it in any way ran counter to their own private judgment, which was in many ways guided to a large degree by their passions and inclinations.[132]

When private judgment is guided by everyone's individual inclinations, everything is up for grabs, and the moral weight of all teaching collapses. That is what happened to the moral issues related to consumerism.

As the West became more industrial (a story with more than a few direct links to the Reformation, which we won't get into here),[133] societal norms became more antagonistic to traditional Christian morality. So, for example, instead of viewing an insatiable desire for material goods as a dangerous vice needing to be controlled, French philosopher Montesquieu extolled it as the very path to happiness.[134] In the same way, atheist philosopher David Hume saw avarice as a "universal passion" that ought to be pursued at all times, for to prevent ourselves from acquiring all the goods and services possible would be to irrationally go against our nature.[135]

As this line of thinking spread, Protestantism simply couldn't hold the line. The Reformation had "undermined the foundations of the only power which was strong enough to keep in check the unbounded avarice and selfishness of man,"[136] and as society grew more and more consumeristic, pressure mounted for Christian ministers not only to ignore the traditional Christian teaching against consumerism, but to justify acquisitiveness and the sins that it fostered. *Sola scriptura* provided a way.

For example, one of the major consequences of the rise of unchecked consumerism was the change in how society viewed the poor. In medieval Catholic culture, poverty was largely viewed with compassion, and even seen as a badge of holiness in the case of those who had voluntarily given up everything for God.[137] The emerging consumeristic world-view, however, did not allow for those categories. After all, if the meaning of life is accumulating goods, it follows that those who refuse to do so are failing at life. Thus, the poor were increasingly viewed with disgrace, considered lazy and deserving of their lot in life. It was in this context that Ralph Waldo Emerson described the typical nineteenth-century Englishman as one who has "pure pride in his wealth and esteems it a final certificate" while "in exact proportion is the reproach of poverty . . . the last term of insult is 'beggar.'"[138]

The contempt for poverty only got worse as Protestant preachers started supporting that notion with Scripture. O'Brien describes the post-Reformation European Protestant attitude toward poverty as "analogous to that displayed by the Jews in the Old Testament, where wealth was regarded as the tangible proof of God's favor, as the recompense of the good

ALL THIS AND HEAVEN TOO

man, and poverty as punishment."[139] Sir Charles Trevelyan, prominent Evangelical and administrator of relief during the Irish Potato Famine of the 1840s, offers a particularly egregious example of this mindset. He considered starvation to be "the judgment of God" on the impoverished Irish."[140]

For scriptural support, theologians used 2 Thessalonians 3:10—"The one who is unwilling to work shall not eat"—and Proverbs 6:9, 19:24, and 26:14–15, which denounce laziness, to blame the poor for their condition[141] It didn't matter that this was entirely contrary to how the Catholic Church had traditionally applied these passages. In the free-for-all that is *sola scriptura*, interpreters could say whatever they wanted.

Early America

In America, this practice was taken to a whole new level, where acquisitiveness was built into the very foundation of the country. Being consumeristic, even at the very beginning of the nation, was part of what it meant to be an American. As Gregory notes,

> The substantive emptiness of the nation's founding documents was possible not only because Americans were strongly shaped by Christian moral assumptions, but also because so many of them had simultaneously departed in practice from the traditional condemnation of avarice. Despite their socially exclusive churches and divergent religious truth claims, late-eighteenth-century free Americans not only shared beliefs about nature as creation and human beings made in God's image. They also had been formed by the Industrial Revolution. So acquisitiveness united them, too, and provided throughout the

nineteenth century an all but axiomatic answer to what they should do with their lives, how they would exercise their liberty, and what the pursuit of happiness entailed, whatever else they might aspire to. "Love of comfort has become the dominant national taste," Tocqueville noted about Americans in the 1830s, adding that "the main current of human passions running in that direction sweeps everything along with it."[142]

Tocqueville also observed that these passions were spurred on by American preachers, who, rather than speak of heaven, were constantly referring to the material blessings of this earth: "It is often difficult to ascertain from their discourses whether the principal object of religion is to procure eternal felicity in the other world, or prosperity in this."[143]

Not every preacher was like this, of course. John Wesley, for example taught clearly and strongly against the evils of mammon[144] and tried to build a Christian community that matched his view of the early Church. However, as David Hempton explains, his experimentation "did not long survive its encounter with basic human acquisitiveness, which, disappointingly for him, proved to be a stronger force in Methodist societies than the social expression of perfect love."[145] Wesley and fellow revivalist George Whitefield were ultimately ignored with regard to their teaching on money and were even attacked with a charge of promoting an early form of Christian communism.[146]

Instead, Methodist preachers, and those from every other denomination, used Scripture to preach about the value of storing up treasures on earth.

For example, a prominent Philadelphia Presbyterian used the Eighth Commandment ("Thou shalt not steal") to pronounce that it was a Christian's duty to increase one's

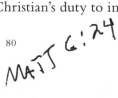
MATT 6:24

"worldly prosperity,"[147] arguing that to not do so would be to rob God of the money-making gifts and talents he had given you. Other preachers focused on the necessity of hard work, using the Bible as a self-help manual that contained principles for making disciplined, industrious, prosperous men. During the 1840s, for example, a Protestant tract titled "True Philosophy for the Mechanic" made its way through working-class America, telling the story of a man who found a "book of philosophy" and followed its principles to material success. He later realized it was the Bible.[148] Thomas Breveridge went so far as to present Jesus as the ideal man of this type, a carpenter who "ennobled labor" forever. "The scriptures give no tolerance to idleness to carelessness respecting our worldly concerns," he sermonized, preaching that the "duty and happiness of man" lies in industry.[149] Pastor Henry Boardman made the supposed link between faith and worldly success explicit in his popular sermon, "Piety Essential to Man's Temporal Prosperity," using as his text 1 Timothy 4:8: "Godliness is profitable unto all things."[150]

This became the accepted approach within Protestant American Christianity. As Richard Pointer summarizes, "Historians have long recognized the growing convergence of Protestant and American middle-class values in the mid-nineteenth century," and they have demonstrated that Evangelical Protestants' ascendancy was due in part "to their willingness to allow their message to be accommodated to the spirit of the culture."[151] An 1857 sermon stated it plainly: "Our object is to baptize the riches of men with the spirit of the gospel."[152]

A particularly eccentric interpretation of the story of the rich man and Lazarus (Luke 16:19–31) shows just how far some were willing to take this goal. In the parable, Jesus compares the eternal fate of a beggar and a wealthy man. The poor man, Lazarus, ends up in heaven, while the rich man begs, to no avail, to be relieved of his misery in hell. In March of 1828, however, a Unitarian minister preached that this story wasn't actually about wealth or poverty at all, and that there was "nothing said in this parable to implicate the character of the rich man, or in favor of Lazarus."[153] Rather, it was an allegory about Jews and Gentiles, so listeners could rest easy in their pursuit of worldly gain, because this parable didn't apply to them.

That's not to say that preachers couldn't find a biblical argument against "mammonism" when it suited their purposes. One of the more interesting and ironic trends in antebellum Southern preaching was the strong denunciation of Northern greed and avarice. Many Southern Evangelicals accused the North of being motivated by sinful industrialist selfishness, and in turn they defended slavery, as we have seen, by linking it to a more virtuous, economically just, biblical way of life. That they could find "biblical" support for slavery in denouncing "unbiblical" economic injustice is one more excellent example of the weakness of *sola scriptura*.

The Catholic position, on the other hand, remained consistent, and presented, in the words of Mark Summers, "a theological challenge to prevailing American beliefs. Catholics challenged the Protestant notions that linked democracy and Christianity, capitalism and Christianity, and the individualism Protestants interpreted from Scripture"[154] As Mark Noll explains, this "amounted to a fundamental assessment of prevailing beliefs and practices that American Protestants, whose main principles were so closely intertwined with the nation's dominant ideologies, could not deliver."[155] Summers concludes:

Northern theologians could not understand Catholic misgivings about the abolitionist movement, with its willingness to break the law for its goals, and Know Nothing roots, while Southern radicals could not abide the Church's sympathy for and identification with the plight and suffering of slaves. Furthermore, while Protestant denominations split along sectional lines and theological interpretations of slavery, even to the point of advocating war, the Catholic Church seemed maddeningly united and suspiciously neutral during the secession crisis.[156]

The Most Popular Religious Movement in America

As we move into the contemporary era, let's take a quick jump forward and start with this fact: the most popular preacher in America right now is Joel Osteen. Pastor of Houston's Lakewood Church, a congregation of 45,000 that meets in a basketball arena, Osteen has the highest-rated religious television show in the country, reaching more than seven million viewers weekly, and is the author of three number-one *New York Times* bestsellers, including what Ross Douthat calls "the most influential popular theology book published this century": *Your Best Life Now: 7 Steps to Living at Your Full Potential*. That book has sold more than eight million copies and has helped solidify Osteen as the king of a worldwide religious empire, one built on a simple proposition: "God wants to increase you financially."[157]

Osteen is a purveyor of a movement within Protestantism known popularly as the *prosperity gospel*, and although he is its biggest name, he is far from alone. Many of the biggest churches and ministries in America now offer a theology of personal health and wealth, assuring their audience that God desires to "bless" them with material comfort.

Pastor Fernando Garay of Charlottesville, Virginia, for example, shows up in his shiny Mercedes–Benz each Sunday to tell his parishioners that Jesus loves money and wants to give them some. "Fight the attack of the devil on my finances! Fight him! We declare financial blessings! Financial miracles this week, NOW NOW NOW!" he shouted on the week that journalist Hanna Rosin visited. "More work! Better work! The best finances!" Rosin recounts that as the message continued, many young men gravitated to the front of the church, jumping and weeping. "On the altar sat some anointing oils, alongside the keys to the Mercedes."[158]

A similar scene plays out all over the country each week. Mega–pastors such as Creflo Dollar, Joyce Meyer, Kirbyjon Caldwell, and Kenneth Copeland preside over event and media empires that have taken over much of American Evangelicalism. According to one analysis, fifty of the largest 260 churches in the country explicitly preach a prosperity gospel and the Trinity Broadcasting Network (TBN), a prosperity gospel outlet, is the world's largest religious network, reaching 175 nations in fourteen languages on thirty-two global networks.[159]

As just one example of how far the prosperity gospel has reached into the congregations, Pew Research recently found that half of all Christian poll respondents believe that wealth will be granted to the faithful.[160]

In *Blessed*, a history of the movement, Kate Bowler notes that millions of Americans have fallen in love with the prosperity gospel and its new kind of preacher: "Charming though not effusive, polished but not slick, these favored few could as easily have appeared on *Piers Morgan Tonight* as behind their megachurch Sunday pulpits."[161] She describes how these preachers have cultivated their fame not only through sold out arenas, but also podcasts, internet streaming, and

BE

daily televisions programming that reaches millions. The
"megachurch ministerial elite" have dominated "not only
religious media networks . . . but secular outlets as well, becoming mainstays on stations like Black Entertainment Television." Their books are on the *New York Times* bestsellers
list and line the religion/inspiration aisles from Walmart to
Barnes & Noble, and at almost any moment, day or night,
the American public can "tune in to see these familiar faces
and a consistent message: God desires to bless you."[162]
Prosperity theology's reach is so broad and lacking in any
common denominator (other than *sola scriptura*) that it ex-
tends beyond denominational and political lines and tran-
scends many of the traditional boundaries within Protestantism. Bowler points out that it "cannot be conflated with
fundamentalism, Pentecostalism, Evangelicalism, the religious right, the so-called black church, or any of the usual
suspects (though it certainly overlaps with each)."[163]
Also, it should be noted that the embrace of avarice on
display here is not limited to churches that are easily rec-
ognizable within the prosperity theology movement. The
consumeristic mindset afflicts many congregations that don't
follow or might even disavow preachers such as Osteen and
would never officially approve of TBN. However, they still
promote consumerism and avarice by promoting the pursuit
of material goods as simply part of the Christian, American
way of life. Douthat, again:

> The stereotype of the prosperity gospel involves a rich
> preacher fleecing the gullible poor, growing fat off their
> donations while promising God-given blessings that nev-
> er materialize. But the reality is just as likely to involve
> ministers who prosper by flattering their upwardly mo-
> bile, American Dreaming congregations, telling them to

keep on striving and praying, because God wants them to keep up with the Joneses next door.[164]

And even in those churches that wouldn't explicitly tell their congregants that God wants them to be rich, it is implied in the *acceptance* of American consumerism. Over the course of my fifty years, I've been to hundreds of Evangelical churches around the country and listened to thousands of sermons, and I don't remember ever hearing a message against the avarice exhibited in American consumerism. I also have a B.A. from an Evangelical Bible college, and an M.A. from a major Evangelical graduate school. Again, I don't remember ever hearing American consumerism questioned within the walls of conservative Evangelical academia.

The bottom line is that a significant percentage of American Protestants live—thanks to *sola scriptura*—as if the plain-sense readings of Jesus' admonition to be on guard against all kinds of greed and that teaching "life does not consist in an abundance of possessions" (Luke 12:15) are simply wrong.

The Rise of the Prosperity Gospel

How did it come to this? Well, today's prosperity preachers can largely trace their roots to a rather obscure early twentieth-century evangelist whose influence has far outpaced his fame: E.W. Kenyon (1867–1948). A pastor loosely affiliated with various Methodist and Baptist groups, Kenyon was a theological entrepreneur at heart, founding two Bible colleges and publishing several books extolling a brand of Christianity that focused on the power of man to get what he wants from God through prayer. These blessings included, of course, material wealth. "God never planned that we should live in poverty, either physical, mental, or spiritual," he wrote in his *Advanced Bible Course*. "He made Israel go to the head of the nations financially. When we go into partnership with him, and we learn his way of doing business, we cannot be failures."[165] Kenyon's work is absolutely saturated in Scripture. His sermons are filled with biblical references to passages such as Ephesians 2:6 and Colossians 3:1, for example, which speak about God raising us up with him.[166] However, Kenyon interpreted these passages in an unorthodox way, one that made the Christian life largely a legal relationship between the believer and God. Within this framework, a person did not so much request things of a merciful God as insist on them as a contractual right. Basically, if we ask for something, God has to give it to us. In this theology, Kate Bower explains, Kenyon "gave priority to the spoken Word above all as the source of God's power." He

taught that Jesus transferred the "Power of Attorney" to all those who use his name. Prayer took on binding legal qualities as believers followed Jesus' formula: "If ye shall ask anything in my name, I will do it" (John 14:14). Kenyon replaced the word "ask" with "demand," since petitioners were entitled to the legal benefits of Jesus' name.[167]

Kenyon himself never became rich or famous, and, to be fair, he doesn't seem to have spent much time demanding wealth or fame from God, either. He was more focused on saving souls. However, his theology persisted, and as the century wore on, it became more and more directly applied to accumulating material wealth.

The primary popularizer of Kenyon's work was a Texas Assemblies of God pastor who became known as the father of the prosperity gospel. Kenneth Hagin drew on Kenyon's work to preach what he called the "Law of Faith," taking the term from Romans 3:27 (KJV): "Where is boasting then? It is excluded. By what law? Of works? Nay: but by the Law of Faith." This law, taught Hagin, entitled believers to use God's power to provide for themselves whatever they hoped for, as long as they asked for it "in Jesus' name."[168] The title of his popular pamphlet, *Write Your Own Ticket with God,* is an apt summary of the theology he was spreading.

That theology picked up steam throughout the forties and fifties, as a growing chorus of preachers advocated prosperity gospel themes, using a variety of biblical passages for support. John 10:10 ("The thief comes only to steal and kill and destroy; I have come that they may have life, and have it to the full.") was popular with speakers at the annual *Voice of Healing* conference, for example,[169] and was also put into heavy rotation by a Tulsa, Oklahoma evangelist named Oral Roberts, who published a periodical called *Abundant Life.* Roberts's favorite verse, though, was 3 John 2: "Beloved, I wish above all things that thou mayest prosper and be in health even as thy soul prospereth" (KJV). He described finding that verse as "the greatest discovery I ever made" and claimed it was the basis for his entire ministry.[170]

That ministry became a media, publishing, and education empire, and Tulsa became a hub of the prosperity gospel movement. Roberts founded Oral Roberts University there in 1963, and Hagin opened Rhema Bible Training Center in Tulsa in 1974. Since that time, tens of thousands of students have been through the doors, including a Houston church-planter named John Osteen and later his son Joel.

The *Word of Faith* movement, as Hagin called it, remained focused on Scripture as its authority. Its central tenet was, in the words of fellow prosperity preacher Kenneth Copeland, that "God's power is in direct relationship with his Word. He has used his Word to release his power. He has sent his Word to us so that we may be in contact with his great power."[171] To support that assertion, Copeland pointed to Jesus, who said, "Whosoever shall say . . . and shall not doubt in his heart, but shall believe that those things which he saith shall come to pass; he shall have whatsoever he saith" (Mark 11:23, KJV) According to prosperity theology, this passage clearly states that Jesus offers us a guarantee: whatever we want—a new car, a bigger house, all the money and comfort we dream of—we can have, if we *say the right words in faith*.[172]

Not everyone agreed with that interpretation, of course. Some denominations even tried to reign in what they considered to be the excesses of their wayward pastors. William Gaston, retired chairman of the Assemblies of God, called the prosperity preachers "lovers of filthy lucre" and lamented that they were drawing congregants away from the true gospel.[173] However, within a *sola scriptura* framework, the denominations were simply unable to hold the preachers accountable.

A.A. Allen is a typical example of the Lone Ranger mentality that could not be penned in. While working as an Assemblies of God pastor, Allen felt called to a media ministry after attending an Oral Roberts tent meeting. When his church refused to let him start a radio program, he left the church and started his own ministry, eventually becoming one of the first evangelists to have a national television show. He kept his affiliation with the Assemblies of God for a while, but when they asked him to withdraw from ministry following a drunk-driving incident, he contemptuously published their request letter, quit the denomination, and kept right on preaching. Indeed, he even added a new wrinkle to his sermons: the assertion that his listeners should avoid the grievous sin of "institutionalized denominationalism."[174]

For his part, Roberts also ran into trouble with his denomination, the Pentecostal Holiness Church, but avoided being ousted in part because he donated $50,000 to their Bible college.[175] He refused to allow his own university to be under their umbrella, however, and later joined the United Methodist Church.[176]

As we saw in chapter 1, that's how it always goes within Protestantism. *Sola scriptura* results in a free-for-all in which preachers can say whatever they want and interpret the Bible to support just about any assertion, and denominations are basically powerless to discipline them or regulate doctrine. There simply is no epistemological or philosophical or theological mechanism for it to be any other way.

Thus, by the late stages of the twentieth century, popular Protestantism was dominated by celebrity preachers with little visible connection to denominations or institutional accountability. This was exacerbated by the advent of television, which took the big-tent revivals of the mid-century into America's living room. During the sixties, seventies, and eighties, "health and wealth" preachers took over the airwaves, with little or no mention of denominational ties.

Rex Humbard, for example, broadcast from his large and lavish "Cathedral of Tomorrow," and in 1970 appeared on more television stations than any other American program.[177] (He also counted among his fans a certain rock-and-roll star named Elvis Presley, and even presided over the King's funeral in 1977.) Humbard's success showed what was possible, and between 1971 and 1981, prosperity preachers jumped from being around 40 percent of religious programming to 83 percent. In the process they created a billion-dollar industry[178] and paved the way for our current cultural milieu.

Throughout the rise of this consumeristic Christianity, preachers have continued to use the Bible to support their claims, becoming ever more creative with their interpretations of Scripture. Benny Hinn and Rod Parsley turned to Genesis 22:24, where God is referred to as *Jehovah Jirah*, the provider. "He is the God of more than enough," explained Parsley. "He gives us the ability to plant, to harvest, and to gather the abundance into the storehouse."[179] These ministers saw prosperity theology as rooted in God's covenant with ancient Israel; favor and riches sprang from faithfulness to that relationship. "In the Old Testament, according to Deuteronomy," Kenneth Hagin explained in his book *Biblical Keys to Financial Prosperity*, "poverty was to come upon God's people if they disobeyed him,"[180] but financial blessing was poured out if they obeyed.

Others audaciously, and implausibly, argued that Jesus himself was a man of great wealth and that we should follow his example. After all, didn't he get expensive gifts when he was born? "As soon as Jesus arrived, that anointing to prosper acted like a magnet, drawing wise men with gifts of gold, frankincense, and myrrh," Creflo Dollar mused. "Those were not cheap gifts, either. Prosperity attached itself to baby Jesus immediately, and that same gift to prosper has been given to us as heirs of Christ."[181]

Reverend C. Thomas Anderson of Living Word Bible Church in Mesa, Arizona, has built on those themes, arguing that even Jesus' undergarments must have been expensive or else the Roman soldiers wouldn't have gambled for them at the cross. Anderson also believes that riding a donkey was the first-century equivalent of "driving a Cadillac," so Jesus' family must have been wealthy.[182] Tom Brown of Word of Life Church in El Paso, Texas adds that John 12 teaches us that Jesus had a "keeper of the money bag," and "the last time I checked, poor people don't have treasurers to take care of their money."[183]

The Sola Scriptura Problem

Now, it is true that American Protestant critiques of consumerism exist,[184] and that there are Protestant communities dedicated to battling avarice. However, as with the issue of slavery, within the *sola scriptura* framework of the Reformation movements, there simply is no authoritative mechanism for saying that any one group or teacher is any more correct than the other. They all can claim the authority of Scripture!

For example, many within Protestantism question the prosperity gospel movement and even explicitly call proponents such as Joel Osteen and Joyce Meyer "false teachers."[185] Often this involves a robust scriptural rebuttal of their books and sermons. John Piper, for example, says that he "abominates the prosperity gospel" and goes into great detail showing from Scripture why it is false.[186] Indeed, he mentions many of the passages we have referenced in this chapter.

But here's the problem. The prosperity gospel preachers also use Scripture to back up their claims! Joel Osteen starts every sermon by holding a Bible over his head and reciting these lines along with the audience: "This is my Bible. I am what it says I am. I have what it says I have. I can do what it says I can do. Today I will be taught the word of God. I boldly confess my mind is alert, my heart is receptive; I'll never be the same. In Jesus' name, God bless you."[187]

Now, Osteen doesn't actually spend much time exegeting biblical passages during his talks, but the point is clear: he is claiming the Bible as the ultimate authority for his message. Should you question whatever he might say, he can fall back on the notion that he is only telling you what the Bible says. He has even published *The Hope for Today Bible*,[188] which contains encouraging commentary notes from Osteen and his wife.

Pastor Garay also likes to use the Bible to support his message, and at offering time often quotes Jesus' words: "Give, and it will be given to you. A good measure, pressed down, shaken together and running over, will be poured into your lap. For with the measure you use, it will be measured to you" (Luke 6:38). During the real estate boom years before the crash of 2008, Garay applied that passage in very specific terms to his congregation, promising that a $100 offering would yield a $10,000 return: "This is not my promise. It is God's promise, and he will make it happen!"[189]

Joyce Meyer goes so far as to claim that "the whole Bible really has one message: 'Obey me and do what I tell you to do, and you'll be blessed.'"[190] That's exactly how Meyer explains her massive fortune, which includes a $10 million private jet. "Here I am, an ex-housewife from Fenton, with a twelfth-grade education. How could anybody look at this and see anything other than God?" she told the *St. Louis Post-Dispatch*.[191]

It does not matter that thousands of words have been published within Evangelical circles denouncing Meyer as a false prophet, charlatan, and heretic.[192] She claims the authority of Scripture with exactly as much validity as her detractors do. Who's to say otherwise? Within a framework of *sola scriptura*, nobody.

This is one big reason why Reformation movements have been ineffective at opposing the increase of greed and consumerism in our world. In the same way that *sola scriptura* was powerless to stop the evil of slavery, and, indeed, ended up providing a divine mandate for it, *sola scriptura* has failed to provide a bulwark against the sins of avarice, and ultimately has clothed them with God's approval.

The rise of prosperity theology and the silence regarding sins of avarice, even from Protestant pulpits not associated with prosperity theology, provide one more example of the negative effects of *sola scriptura*. Far from helping Christians address or contain the sinful consumerism of the industrial West, it has actually made it worse by giving it divine sanction—mixing temporal prosperity into Jesus' message of eternal salvation. Yes, many Protestants find the message of the prosperity gospel unbiblical and call its proponents false teachers.[193] That doesn't really matter, though. Within a *sola scriptura* framework, no Protestant has any more right to offer a "correct" interpretation than any other. If the Bible—and your own personal interpretation of it—is all you have, you can make it say anything you want.

Do this with enthusiasm, charisma, and salesman savvy, and if you get enough followers it can even be your own ticket to a big mansion and a Mercedes in the garage!

THE CATHOLIC DIFFERENCE

One of the most visible consequences of the sins of avarice is the breakdown of the family, which a consumeristic lifestyle accelerates. Couples and families that are always rushing and striving to support lifestyles based on acquisition and constant activity don't spend restful time together interacting as humans. Chronically tired, what little free time they *can* find is usually spent "vegging out" in front of a screen. As Fr. Timothy Vavareck writes, "It is a lifestyle inhospitable to the type of time and personal interaction that is truly restful and restorative. It is a world in which prayer, the spiritual life, the Church, and God are often numbered among the myriad of events that must be fit into daily life instead of taking their rightful place as the hinges upon which daily life turns." Consumerism plays upon fallen human nature by conditioning us to feed our desires, resulting in the never-ending pursuit of a lifestyle that is inherently disordered. "Those who have given over to a consumeristic lifestyle cannot give proper priority to rest, recreation, joy, or prayer. They simply do not have the time, energy, or security to do so."[194]

What is the solution? According to Fr. Vavareck, the families in his parish that are most successful against consumerism have one thing in common: they cultivate *virtue*. How do they do that? The same way it has always been done: by practicing asceticism. Specifically, Fr. Vavareck recommends three practices that "confront the vice of consumerism" and "foster the temperance and justice needed to overcome the false desires" it arouses: the penitential life, the honoring of the sabbath, and the offering of the tithe.

1) The *penitential life* consists of three types of actions: fasting (or self-denial), prayer, and almsgiving (or works of mercy). Each of these battles the vices of consumerism. Through the practice of self-denial, "the Christian turns away from the inessential desires of his will and his flesh, being content with God's will for his life." In prayer, Christians seek "an ever-deeper communion with God and the grace to persevere in the narrow path of love." And by giving alms and practicing works of mercy, "a Christian not only shares material goods with others, he pours himself out on their behalf."

Fr. Vavarek notes that by its very nature, this kind of life turns a believer away from the selfish pursuit of mammon, humanizes the society in which he lives, and brings hope to a fallen world. "Such a Christianity is neither an opiate nor a revolution; it is a prophetic witness radiating from the Church which transforms her members and the whole world."[195]

2. *Honoring the sabbath* "carves out space for God and others, a time for resting from labor, acquisition, and consumption to enjoy personal relationships and the fruits of the earth."[196] By properly keeping the Lord's Day to rest and worship, we align ourselves to God's calendar and God's economy, realigning ourselves with his perspective. This is essential in a culture that lives and breathes consumerism.

3. Finally, *tithing* has a similar effect to honoring the Sabbath, says Fr. Vavareck, who cites the traditional tithe amount of 10 percent. "In order to give 10 percent to God's work, people cannot be spending everything on themselves," he says, rightly noting that for our typical "overextended" Western consumers to find that 10 percent in their budgets, their "entire lifestyle would have to change. The monthly budget would need to revolve to a certain extent around the tithe. Thus, a limit on spending would be established by rendering first to God what is his."[197] This is a powerful antidote to consumerism!

Now, a Protestant might say that each of these virtue-builders can be, and are, practiced by non-Catholics as well, and of course that is correct. Asceticism can be found in all Christian communities. Many Evangelicals *do* tithe (how else would prosperity pastors get rich?). But only Catholicism has the interpretative authority, bound up with its long tradition of embracing holy poverty and placing material goods at the service of God and the poor, to place ascetical values before the faithful in every place and age without corruption of the message.

It also has a *practical* authority over its flock when it comes to practices and precepts that promote virtuous habits. Take Mass obligations, for instance. When I first heard, while I was still a Protestant, that it was considered a sin for Catholics not to go to Mass on Sunday, I couldn't believe it. How could they be so legalistic and petty? But now I see it. This isn't a legalistic infringement on freedom. It is the path to freedom. God, through his Church, has graciously provided us the way to holiness and happiness, and the directions for how to accomplish it. These directions aren't optional, as least not if you want to be the type of person God intended you to be. Knowing human nature, the Church does not make them optional, but uses its authority to direct us to follow them.

And although some groups within Protestantism might talk about building virtue as something that is "not optional," *sola scriptura* simply does not provide the authority to enforce that truth. This leaves Protestants much more vulnerable to destructive cultural forces such as consumerism.

This is especially true when we consider the broader theological context in which the Catholic Church offers its rules. Not only does the Church clearly condemn the evils of consumerism, as we have seen, but it offers a beautiful alternative option: the path of holy poverty. Displayed perhaps most famously by St. Francis of Assisi, but practiced by religious throughout Christian history, this tradition completely rejects the pursuit and accumulation of earthly goods, welcoming poverty as a way to get closer to God, who alone provides our daily bread.

Indeed, to say that those who embark on this journey lack anything is to misunderstand their position. They aren't missing anything in that they don't see worldly things as worth pursuing. Temporal trinkets are nothing in comparison to God, and, in fact, get in the way of God and our necessary attitude of dependence on his Providence. To say that one who has taken vows of poverty lacks something is like saying that a prisoner who is released from jail now lacks the walls that kept him hemmed in. Those who choose holy poverty do so because they understand that God is better than all the petty things worldly wealth offers, and they see that worldly wealth hinders them from God. In contrast to the view we have described in much of this chapter, which views wealth as a sign of God's blessing and poverty as a sign of God's disfavor, the Catholic Church affirms that a voluntary embrace of poverty can be both instrument and sign of our intimacy with God.[198]

Would that more would heed that call, as such holiness has been starkly lacking in our consumeristic culture. As harmful as the evils of consumerism have been, however, I actually think there is a category of sins that *sola scriptura* has enabled that have been even more destructive to the world. That will be the subject of our last chapter.

CHAPTER 4

SEXUAL DEVOLUTION

THE SIN THAT BECAME THE CENTRAL FACT OF OUR TIME

The Most Important Event of Recent History

The twentieth century was filled with world-shattering events. Wars. Revolutions. Technological breakthroughs. From the fall of the Ottoman Empire to the development of the internet, it was a century that changed everything, and its consequences continue to affect each of us today.

One particular twentieth-century development stands alone as what Mary Eberstadt called the "central fact of our time" in that "it is hard to think of any other whose demographic, social, behavioral, and personal fallout has been as profound."[199] Albert Mohler goes even further: "I cannot imagine any development in human history, after the Fall, that has had a greater impact on human beings," he told the *New York Times*.[200] Popes St. Paul VI and St. John Paul II connected this event directly to the breakdown of the family, the sexual objectification of women, the increase in adultery, divorce, and abortion, the embrace of homosexuality, and the rise of transgenderism. What historical development am I talking about? The widespread moral acceptance of contraception. As Jennifer Fulwiler says of her pre-Catholic days, "I never even knew you could be against contraception. I mean, who is anti-contraception?" Like most people of our generation, she thought contraception was a universal good, "just something all people need . . . a necessary resource, like air or water."[201] That had been my approach as well. Jen grew up atheist and I grew up Protestant, but we both unquestioningly accepted contraception as a beneficial, nay, *essential* part of life, and assumed it had always been that way. Indeed, as Jen explains, when she first heard that the Catholic Church opposed it, she thought it was an urban legend.

But what we both would come to realize is that not only does the Catholic Church oppose contraception, but so did essentially all Christians until very recently. As we will see in this chapter, the story of how Protestants came to reject that teaching is another example of the utter failure of *sola scriptura*, one that has had disastrous consequences.

A Unity of Thought

Amid all the doctrinal development and disagreement in Church history, Christian teaching about contraception in the first 1900 years is remarkable for its unanimity and continuity. From the early Church through the early twentieth century, attempting to stop the sexual act from being procreative was considered a grave sin by essentially all believers, everywhere.

In the face of gnostic heresies that devalued marriage and the natural functions of the body, Church Fathers such as Clement of Alexandria, Justin Martyr, and John Chrysostom, for example, all affirmed that sex was good and was intended for begetting children.[202] St. Augustine echoed these themes in several of his writings, including *On the Good of Marriage* and *Marriage and Concupiscence*, in which he compared using contraception with committing adultery.[203] He also spoke about contraception in his commentary on Genesis 38, which contains the story in which Onan "wasted his seed on the ground" rather than risk conceiving a child with his wife. Augustine wrote, "Sexual intercourse even with a lawful wife is unlawful and shameful, if the offspring of children is prevented. This is what Onan, the son of Juda, did and on that account God put him to death."[204]

That was the accepted view throughout the Middle Ages and it didn't really change at the Reformation, either. Indeed, Martin Luther was perhaps even more vehemently opposed to contraception than his forbears. In his commentary on Genesis, he wrote, "Onan must have been a most malicious and incorrigible scoundrel. This is a most disgraceful sin. It is far more atrocious than incest and adultery . . . it was a most disgraceful crime . . . he deserved to be killed by God."[205]

For his part, John Calvin turned to Genesis 1:28, where God commands Adam and Even to be fruitful and multiply. Calvin argues that this is the only command God gave in the garden that was still active after the fall and was therefore uniquely important. He added that this "pure and lawful method of increase, which God ordained from the beginning, remains firm; this is that law of nature which common sense declares to be inviolable."[206] He also wrote, "The voluntary spilling of semen outside of intercourse between man

and woman is a monstrous thing. Deliberately to withdraw from coitus in order that semen may fall on the ground is doubly monstrous. For this is to extinguish the hope of the race and to kill before he is born the hoped-for offspring."[207]
Later Protestants, including American Evangelicals, remained solidly in line with received orthodoxy on this matter. Cotton Mather, for example, warned against the self-polluting crime of "onanism,"[208] as did John Wesley, who proclaimed that "those sins that dishonor the body and defile it are very displeasing to God and evidences of vile affections." Those that practice them "destroy their own souls."[209]

American Protestant rejection of contraception was so strong, in fact, that near the end of the nineteenth century, as battles over public morality raged around the country, Puritan activists such as Anthony Comstock were its most outspoken opponents. A postal inspector and founder of the New York Society for the Suppression of Vice, Comstock worked tirelessly to rid society of practices he considered evil. His crowning achievement in this area was the passage of the "Comstock Laws," a set of federal statutes that made it illegal to send obscene items through the mail. Among the banned obscenities: pornographic literature, abortifacients, and contraceptives. Comstock believed (and the twentieth century confirmed that he was correct, as we will see) that porn, abortion, and contraception were intimately linked, and that they were having a devastating effect on the population. He was particularly concerned about children, and saw his mission as having been "assigned by the Great Commander to constantly face some of the most insidious and deadly forces of evil that Satan is persistently aligning against the integrity of the children of the present age."[210]

From today's perspective, support for the Comstock Laws and opposition to contraception came from an astoundingly wide cross section of the country. The *New York Times* praised Comstock for sustaining "the cause of morality" and for going after "those wretches who are debauching the youth of our country and murdering women and unborn babies."[211] No less a showman than P.T. Barnum helped move the Comstock bill through the legislature.[212] Comstock even had presidents on his side. Theodore Roosevelt hated birth control, stating that "it is the one sin for which the penalty is national death"[213] and that those who practice it "should be an object of contemptuous abhorrence by all healthy people."[214] And Woodrow Wilson appointed Comstock to lead the American Delegation to the 1915 International Purity Conference, held that year in San Francisco (if you can believe that) with more than 4,000 delegates.

Comstock died later that year, largely having accomplished what he set out to do. He had gone "further than any pope or canonist"[215] in penalizing the trade in birth control devices and information, making it dangerous "to even discuss contraception in print,"[216] and for that he was a hero to many.

So what happened? How did we go from popular Comstock Laws and International Purity Conferences to a culture in which I grew up not knowing it was even possible to oppose contraception, a culture that is so pornified the parents like me struggle to keep our daughters from being "sexted" by their schoolmates?[217] The answer is that even by 1915, developments had been underway that would crumble our moral foundations, and their total collapse was not far off. Again, the principle of *sola scriptura* was a major factor.

Luther's Flaw

Luther might have agreed with traditional Catholic dogma regarding the sinfulness of contraception, but by separating himself from Church authority and leaning on his own understanding of Scripture, he opened himself up to error in all kinds of related issues.

For example, one of Luther's main contentions with the Church was the issue of priestly celibacy. Luther believed that taking a vow of chastity and dedicating oneself to the service of God was a sin against the scriptural command to "be fruitful and multiply" (Gen. 1:28). He wanted all nuns and priests instead to deny their vows, get married, and have large families. As Allan Carlson explains, Luther took God's charge to Adam and Eve and twisted it into something that historical Christianity couldn't recognize:

> Luther elevated marriage to "the highest religious order on earth," concluding that "we may be assured that man and woman should and must come together in order to multiply." He stressed that it was "not a matter of free choice . . . but a natural and necessary thing, that whatever is a man must have a woman and whatever is a woman must have a man." He urged that the convents be emptied, emphasizing that "a woman is not created to be a virgin, but to conceive and bear children." Indeed, Luther's marital pronatalism had no restraints: wives ought to be continually pregnant, he said, because "this is the purpose for which they exist."[218]

Subsequently, many Protestant pastors did their best to live up to Luther's instruction, serving their flocks while also growing families and taking care of their wives and kids. However, as Scripture and the Catholic Church have always recognized, that arrangement comes with extra pressure,[219] and by the early twentieth century, amid the continuing fallout of the Industrial Revolution, Protestant groups were noticing a disturbing trend: their pastors were not having as many kids as they once did. For example, an Anglican census taken in 1911 showed that clergymen were only having an average of 2.3 children, well below the 5.2 they had in 1874.[220] Similarly, the Lutheran Church Missouri Synod found that their clerical families had gone from an average of 6.5 offspring in 1890 to 3.7 in 1920.[221]

Why? From outward appearances, the obvious answer was that these pastors were using some sort of measures to restrict pregnancy and birth.

The Descent

They were not alone; family size was dropping among lay-people as well. The fact is, even as Comstock Laws were enacted and Protestant leaders at least paid lip service to traditional sexual morality during the late nineteenth and early twentieth centuries, there was a strong undercurrent of rebellion starting to flow, and a contraceptive mentality was on the rise. It was driven by three main tributaries.

First, the consumerism we talked about in chapter 3 had begun to dampen the desire for large families. As more time and energy went to making money and accumulating things, less went to getting married and having children. Already in 1887, president of the Evangelical Alliance William Dodge decried "the loose opinions as to family ties, the increased licentiousness, the materialism of the age, the absorption in money-making," and "the increased luxury and enervation in many classes" as grave causes for concern.[222]

Second, the licentiousness Dodge mentioned in 1887 only got worse in the ensuing decades. Sexual experimentation and license got a major boost, for example, when Sigmund Freud published *The Interpretation of Dreams* in 1900. In it he argued that the sex drive was the most important aspect of human life. Sex was so essential, in fact, that not to gratify this primal urge would do severe damage to mind and body. In Freud's view, sexual satisfaction was essential to happiness and health, and abstinence must be avoided at all costs. Although critics in Europe were initially skeptical, Freud found a much more welcoming audience in America.[223] His followers there, which included many young women, eagerly sought to "lose their inhibitions" and find fulfillment in sexual pleasure. Freud disciple William Reich even taught that if everyone released enough sexual energy, it would lead to a global revolution usher in world peace and security.[224] (Promiscuous sex did usher in a global revolution, but it certainly didn't lead to peace, security, or anything resembling real happiness. More on that later.)

The third major factor in the move toward acceptance of contraception was a growing concern about overpopulation. This displayed itself in two major ways. First, middle- and upper-class white Protestants were moved to limit the size of their own families based on the theory, put forth by English clergyman Thomas Malthus, that the world would run out of food if they didn't. Second, those same middle- and upper-class white Protestants expressed increasing alarm that they were being overrun by non-white, lower-class, non-Protestants. In the United States, they were especially concerned about the growing numbers of immigrant Catholics, very few of whom were taking any steps to limit *their* family size. Articles from the era lament the fact that "Rome is conquering North America!" and the "spirit of Protestantism is in decay."

At once, Protestantism was pursuing and lamenting the decrease of family size. One headline from the era proclaimed,

"Protestantism Falling Behind Through Unproductive Marriages," and Meyrick Booth, writing in the *Hibbert Journal* in 1915, declared that "modern Protestantism is now (in practice if not in theory) virtually identified with a very extreme type of Malthusianism . . . The cream of its human material is suffering gradual extinction."[225] You might think that the solution to the "extinction of Protestantism" would be to match its practice to its doctrine. After all, contraception was still "officially" considered immoral; if Protestants stopped practicing it and had bigger families, the problem would be solved.

Admittedly, some did make this point. The Lambeth Conference of Anglican bishops in 1908 "earnestly call[ed] upon all Christian people to discountenance the use of all artificial means of restriction as demoralizing to character and hostile to national welfare."[226] The official magazine of the Lutheran Church Missouri Synod accused the recently formed Birth Control Federation of America of spattering the country with "slime," and Walter Maier, founding preacher of the Lutheran Hour radio program, called contraceptives "the most repugnant of modern aberrations, representing a twentieth-century renewal of pagan bankruptcy."[227]

Such admonitions, however, simply didn't gain much traction. Protestants chose not only to keep practicing contraception but to embrace the growing *eugenics* movement that would ultimately lead them to seek to force contraception (and sterilization) on the communities they didn't like in order keep those populations in check. As usual, *sola scriptura* played a role.

Darwinism, Eugenics, and Protestantism

One of the first to lay a foundation for "Christian" eugenics was Josiah Strong. A Congregationalist pastor and chair of the Evangelical Alliance for the United States, Strong became a leading voice for Social Darwinism and American imperialism, writing books such as *Our Country: Its Possible Future and Its Present Crisis* (1885) and *The New Era, or The Coming Kingdom* (1893). In these works, Strong argued that the world's future depended on the rise and rule of the "Anglo-Saxon race" and that it was their God-given calling to fight back any threats that stood in their way, including those from Catholicism, Mormonism, Socialism, and immigration. "This race is destined to dispossess many weaker ones, assimilate others, and mold the remainder until . . . it has Anglo-Saxonized mankind," he wrote.[228] In this way, the world would become "Christianized."[229]

How would the Anglo-Saxon race dispossess the weaker groups? Strong presented what he considered a thoroughly loving, "Christian" strategy: by following Jesus' command to "go and make disciples of all nations, baptizing them in the name of the Father and of the Son and of the Holy Spirit" (Matt. 28:19). Through the teaching of the faith, Strong believed, high-culture Protestant Christians would "civilize" the low-culture weaker races. As the "less-cultivated" learned the values of Western Protestantism, such as how to practice better hygiene and build better houses, they would also embrace another trait as part of the package: less fecundity.[230] It was a sociological truth of the time, the reasoning went, that the more "advanced" a society became, the less offspring it would produce. The bottom line: fewer undesirables in the world for Strong to have to worry about Christianizing.

Strong tried to package his remedy as a kindness, but it was, of course, just the ruthless social application of Darwin's recently published theory of human descent, the popular version of which summed up life as "the survival of the fittest." Strong believed that Anglo-Saxons were the fittest race, and should therefore survive. He simply added a Christian gloss to it.

Other Protestant churchmen of the time made this connection more explicit and more "biblical." Charles Kingsley, for example, wrote that

> physical science is proving more and more the immense importance of race. . . she is proving more and more how the more favored race exterminates the less favored, or at least expels it . . . The natural theology of the future must take count of these tremendous and even painful facts . . . Scripture has taken count of them already . . . Its sense of the reality and importance of descent is so intense, that it speaks of a whole tribe or whole family by the name of its common ancestor, and the whole nation of the Jews is Israel to the end.[231]

Kingsley goes on to state that the central historic fact of the New Testament, save one, is the destruction of that race of Jews because God found it wanting. He even quotes a prophecy of Jesus to back up this theory: "The kingdom of God shall be taken from you and given to a nation bringing forth the fruits hereof" (Matt. 21:43).

This false idea that the kingdom of God would arrive on earth as a particular race of people gained ascendancy, and with its sketchy "scriptural" warrant made possible because of *sola scriptura*, became a major justification for Christian support of the burgeoning eugenics movement. It only got worse from there.

In 1925, for example, Philip Osgood of Minneapolis preached a Mother's Day sermon called *The Refiner's Fire* that became a national sensation and won first prize in a sermon contest held by the American Eugenics Society.[232] Using Malachi 3:3 as his base text, Osgood proclaimed that the kingdom of God required genetically fit believers, and that just as "the impurities of dross and alloy are purified out of our silver" before it can "be taken into the hands of the craftsman for whom the refining was done," so God's work on earth will not be finished "until the insane and criminal specimens of humanity are removed.[233] He even invoked Jesus as the model eugenicist, calling him the "refiner" of men who "was superlatively concerned to better the qualities of human living."[234]

Allan Carlson summarizes some of the other ways Protestant ministers of the time misappropriated Scripture to support eugenics:

[Some] preachers focused on the Old Testament. They noted the attention paid to genealogy by the Hebrews. "Eugenic matings" included Abraham and Sarah, Isaac and Rebekah, Jacob and Rachael, and Moses with the daughter of the priest of Midian. Isaac became "the eugenic son" of Abraham. Joseph, another exemplary "eugenic son," had to struggle against his "mongrel" brothers, the products of polygamy. These preachers also stressed the importance of the genealogy of Jesus, found in two of the Gospels. As one asked, "Can we, after beholding that stream of life coming down from the eternal, enriched by the struggles of all the noblest and purest lives of the past, can we destroy that divine image . . . or shall we transmit it, pure and undefiled, in all its richness to the coming generations?"[235]

The Prophetess of Sexual Vice

So traditional Christian morality was under attack from consumerism, increased sexual promiscuity, and the eugenics movement, and more and more Protestant pastors, ill-equipped to respond because of *sola scriptura*, were well on their way to a full-throated embrace of contraception. Now when I say that Christian morality was under attack, I mean that quite literally. This was an organized, well-funded movement with the express purpose of bringing clergy on board with a Satanic scheme that would ultimately undermine the family and destroy millions of lives. And the woman at the forefront was the world's foremost promoter of contraception, the founder of Planned Parenthood, Margaret Sanger.

Sanger personified the vices we have been documenting.

Regarding sex, she was a follower of Freud who had multiple affairs and firmly believed in the almost mystical power of the orgasm. In her book *The Pivot of Civilization*, Sanger views sex as a creative energy that we need to release through our "reproductive glands" and the more we do, the higher our "mental and psychic development" will be.[236]

Regarding eugenics, she was a hard-core Darwinist who believed in eradicating the "feeble-minded." She wrote that "the most urgent problem of today is how to limit and discourage the over-fertility of the mentally and physically defective," and that "possibly drastic and Spartan methods may be forced upon American society if it continues complacently to encourage the chance and chaotic breeding that has resulted from our stupid, cruel sentimentalism."[237] When she launched the *Birth Control Review* in 1917, the tag line on the masthead read "Birth Control: To Create a Race of Thoroughbreds."

Somewhat ironically, Sanger had been driven to activism in part because of the Comstock Laws. She had seen her own mother struggle to raise eleven children, and then worked as a midwife and nurse among the poor families of lower Manhattan. "The menace of another pregnancy hung like a sword over the head of every poor woman I came in contact with," she claimed,[238] so she had searched for some literature on contraception. When she couldn't find any, thanks to Comstock, she became his biggest nemesis. Sanger began writing a weekly sex education column in a socialist New York paper, which he promptly banned. Then, in 1914, after launching her own magazine, *The Woman Rebel*, she was indicted on indecency charges and had to flee to Europe, where she remained in exile until Comstock died the following year.

Upon her return, Sanger worked tirelessly to make contraception legal and culturally accepted. She opened the country's first "birth control" clinic in 1916 and began publishing again. In 1920, she released the book *Women and the New Race*, and the next year she gathered advocates together for the first American Birth Control Conference, which would become the starting point for the American Birth Control League (the predecessor organization to Planned Parenthood.) Her goal in it all was to argue for a "new sex morality" far different from the old one based on "ignorance and submission."[239]

That "old morality" was, of course, traditional Christian morality. As R. Marie Griffith explains, "Sanger knew that this morality threatened church doctrine and she proclaimed it proudly: 'Let it be realized that this creation of new sex ideals is a challenge to the church.'"[240] However, Sanger was smart enough to realize that not every church was equally strong or equally a threat, and that some churches could actually be convinced to change their doctrine. She also knew that if she could get those churches on board, her task of changing the morality of the nation would be far easier. As such, for the rest her career she pursued a very specific strategy: fight the Catholics but woo the Protestants.

Not only were Protestants much more likely to change their views, but Sanger could play on their anti-Catholicism to encourage that shift.[241] If the Catholics were against contraception, after all, doesn't that already make it a suspect position? In this way, Sanger relentlessly pursued Protestant support. As Griffith explains, "Sanger knew that Protestant leaders and their denominations were a crucial constituency that needed to be lobbied, and she did so with gusto, attending countless church conventions in order to reach leaders directly and corresponding with them by mail, as she urged them to reach out to fellow ministers within their own denominations."[242]

One of Sanger's favorite themes while addressing these leaders was anti-Catholicism. She especially focused on the idea that contraception was a Catholic idea, and to agree with their teaching on this topic was to submit to Rome. This was the time of the KKK, a period of intense anti-Catholicism in America, and Sanger played to those prejudices. She wrote in *Birth Control Review*, "All who resent this sinister Church Control of life and conduct . . . must now choose between Church Control and Birth Control. You must make a declaration of independence, of self-reliance, or submit to the dictatorship of the Roman Catholic hierarchy . . . a dictatorship of celibates."[243]

Sadly but predictably, this strategy worked.[244] As we will see, Sanger was very effective at wooing the Bible Alone crowd and getting them to give up their traditional teaching, and this was the development she needed to fuel the Sexual Revolution. Without the acquiescence of so many Protestant groups to contraception, it would never have taken off the way it did.

Preaching for Planned Parenthood

One of the first Christian voices for contraception came, in another irony of history, from the Young Men's Christian Organization (YMCA)—the very group where Comstock got his start. Under the leadership of eugenics promoter Sherwood Eddy, the YMCA began offering classes in "responsible parenthood" for the "betterment of the race" as early as 1910, and later promoted Sanger's book *Happiness in Marriage*.[245] Eddy believed that this teaching was entirely in line with the "social gospel" that he claimed Jesus taught in the Bible. According to this interpretation, eugenics was one way to fulfill the Great Commandment of Matthew 22:37: Love the Lord your God with all your heart and love your neighbor as yourself.[246]

Harry Emerson Fosdick was another coup for Sanger. As pastor of the prestigious Riverside Church in New York, Fosdick counted among his parishioners one John D. Rockefeller, who would go on to become one of the world's most influential birth control advocates. Fosdick also served on the board of the American Eugenics Society and gained national media coverage with a pro-contraception sermon in 1927, in which he claimed that it would help strengthen marriage. In 1929, Fosdick published the article "Religion and Birth Control," which Sanger reprinted and distributed as a pamphlet.[247]

How did Fosdick justify his denial of traditional morality? He appealed to the Bible, of course. Interestingly, even though he interpreted Scripture from the perspective of a theological liberal who rejected a "fundamentalist" approach to Scripture,[248] he nonetheless justified his sexual ethic with a direct appeal to it. He argued:

> Repeatedly one runs on verses like this: "It was said to them of old time. . . but I say unto you" [Matt. 5:27];

"God, having of old time spoken unto the fathers in the prophets by divers portions and in divers manners, hath at the end of these days spoken unto us in his Son" [Heb.1:1]; "The times of ignorance therefore God overlooked; but now he commandeth men that they should all everywhere repent" [Acts 17:30]; and over the doorway of the New Testament into the Christian world stand the words of Jesus: "When he, the Spirit of truth, is come, he will guide you into all truth" [John 16:13].[249]

Fosdick's approach *used the Bible to undermine the Bible.* In requiring him to make Scripture the rule for his beliefs but allowing him to interpret Scripture privately, *sola scriptura* effectively empowered him to reject portions of Scripture he didn't agree with.

It was an approach that was working for Margaret Sanger. Other denominational publications also jumped on board the contraception train, including the Methodist *Christian Advocate* and the Baptist *Watchman-Examiner,* printing articles critical of Catholicism's evil authoritarianism and disregard for the future of the race.[250] At the same time, Sanger was working with pastors across the Protestant spectrum, such as Unitarian John Haynes Holmes of the Community Church of New York and the Rev. James Oesterling, superintendent of the Inner Mission Society of the Evangelical Lutheran Synod of Baltimore (who complained to Sanger about "colleagues who practice but do not preach birth control").[251]

It was the Anglicans who first made it official, though. Sanger had been working on them hard, she explains in her autobiography, even to the point of corresponding with bishops' wives about how best to get their husband "thoroughly enlightened" on the subject.[252] At the 1930 Lambeth

Conference—a regular gathering of Anglican bishops—her work paid off. On a vote of 193–67, with forty-six abstaining, the bishops approved a resolution stating that in some cases where there is a "clearly-felt moral obligation to limit or avoid parenthood, and where there is a morally sound reason for avoiding complete abstinence, other methods may be used."[253]

The language was modest, but the floodgates were open. Just a few months later, the Federal Council of Churches of Christ's Committee on Home and Marriage became the first American group to formally acquiesce to the spirit of the times. Made up of Methodist, Presbyterian, Congregational, and Brethren denominations, the FCCC issued a statement defending birth control and urging the repeal of laws prohibiting contraceptive devices.[254] Sanger was thrilled, calling the FCCC statement "epoch-making" and calling the day of the decision "the most significant one in the history of the birth control movement."[255] Looking back later, she saw that these early statements from Lambeth and the FCCC would inevitably "lead the way toward the crystallization of a universal Protestant acceptance of the moral necessity of birth control."[256]

Indeed. Certainly, there were some initial Protestant objections to Lambeth and the FCCC, but over the next few decades dissent largely evaporated, especially as the postwar baby boom gave way to new fears of overpopulation and an increasing number of women entering the workforce further dampened family size.

Again, the reinterpretation of Scripture fueled the movement. Luther had pointed to Genesis 1:28 to support his opposition to contraception; now Albert Rehwinkel, one of the leading Lutheran theologians of the mid-twentieth century, concluded that the father of the Reformation was simply wrong. "Be fruitful and multiply" wasn't a *command* of God, Rehwinkel argued, but merely an optional blessing. In his book *Planned Parenthood and Birth Control in the Light of Christian Ethics*, Rehwinkel also stated that he could find "nowhere" in Scripture "a clear and definite statement on . . . which a positive law or rule making the use of contraceptives in marriage a sinful procedure could be established."[257] According to *sola scriptura*, who could say that Luther was right and Rehwinkel wrong?

Another popular line of thinking focused on the latter part of that Genesis passage, where God grants people "dominion over the earth." We are decision-making agents, this argument went, and God wants us to be good stewards of what he had given us. Part of this responsibility involves deciding how many children we should have *and* deciding how best to go about achieving that number; and within that framework, contraception is fine.[258] Exemplifying this camp was the Augustana Evangelical Lutheran Church, which went so far as to warn that "unrestrained production of children" might be considered "sinful and selfish," an "indulgence of the lusts of the flesh."

By the late 1950s, birth control was approved by leaders across the Protestant spectrum, from mainstreamers like Reinhold Niebuhr, Karl Barth, and Paul Tillich to Evangelicals such as Harold J. Ockenga and the editorial board of *Christianity Today*, which strangely opined that Christians could follow their consciences in this matter because the Bible does not discuss birth control, as "avoidance of parenthood was unheard of in biblical times."[259] Even Billy Graham was on board, telling the *New York Times* that there is nothing in Scripture that bars the responsible use of birth control and that it provided an answer to the "terrifying and tragic" problem of overpopulation.[260]

The Sixties

With the ongoing repeal of Comstock Laws and the FDA's approval of the birth control pill in 1960, the Sexual Revolution kicked into overdrive. We won't take time to go into all of the various factors at play or all the various players (Betty Friedan, Alfred Kinsey, Helen Gurley Brown, Hugh Hefner, and many others), but suffice to say it was a cultural explosion that propelled society toward sexual chaos and the collapse of the family at breakneck speed.[261]

Sadly, the Protestant arguments in support of contraception kept pace. In 1961, the National Council of Churches held a truly egregious "North American Conference on Church and Family," in which the lineup of speakers

formed a veritable "Who's Who" of sexual radicalism. Lester Kirkendall said that America had "entered a sexual economy of abundance," where contraception would allow unrestrained sexual experimentation without the burden of children. Wardell Pomeroy of the [Kinsey] Institute of Sex Research explained how the new science of sexology required the abandonment of all old moral categories. Psychologist Evelyn Hooker praised the healthily sterile lives of homosexuals. Planned Parenthood's Mary Calderone made the case for universal contraceptive use, while colleague Alan Guttmacher urged the reform of America's "mean spirited" anti-abortion laws.[262]

In the keynote, J.C. Wynn of Colgate Divinity School dismissed previous Protestant teaching on the family and sexuality as "depressingly platitudinous," "comfortably dull," and even a regrettable example of "works righteousness."[263]

The more conservative wing of American Protestantism was not quite so zealous but it still got on board, even adding more "biblical" arguments to the existing repertoire. *Christianity Today*, for example, was relatively quiet on the issue during the early sixties, but later in the decade it published several pro-contraception articles, including John Warwick Montgomery's "How to Decide the Birth Control Question" in 1966. Montgomery claimed to distinguish between how Catholics and secularists approach the issue—by using natural law arguments—and how Protestants do, by relying on Scripture alone. Natural law arguments are unreliable, he said, but if we go to the Bible, it will give us the answer. What is that answer? For Montgomery, the key was to realize that Genesis 1:28, on which so much pro-fecundity theology is built, has been superseded by Ephesians 5:22–32, which quotes Genesis in light of the new covenant in Christ. He writes:

> Understood in the light of New Testament fulfillment, marriage cannot be regarded simply as a means ("Be fruitful, and multiply, and replenish the earth") or unqualifiedly as an end ("They shall be one flesh"). Rather, it is seen as an analogy—indeed, as the best human analogy—of the relationship between Christ and his Church.[264]

Since Christ's bond to the Church was a "*total* love relation, not just a means to an end, so one must not view marriage simply as a procreative function. Where birth control can contribute to 'subduing the earth' in order to achieve a better total human relationship, it is not to be condemned."[265]

Montgomery never mentions why *his* biblical answer differs from that of so many other biblical Protestants in history, or why his is the better one. (And he exhibits a ridiculously shallow and incorrect understanding of Catholic natural law arguments.[266]) That didn't matter much to his fans, though, who made that piece a reference point for Evangelical theological justification of contraception.[267]

Christianity Today followed that up in 1968 with an entire edition dedicated to contraception and abortion. In the cover story, "The Old Testament and Birth Control," Bruce K. Waltke of Dallas Theological Seminary offers an extensive biblical justification for contraception, referencing passages from Genesis, Leviticus, Psalms, Deuteronomy, and Ecclesiastes. This includes an explanation of the Onan story (Gen. 38:8–10), and he admits that traditional interpretations of that passage present "valid objections" and a "difficulty that must be faced." However, he sees himself as well up to the challenge, arguing that Onan's sin was not restricting conception, but rather the fact that he "used his brother's wife with no respect for her personality and dignity, and without brotherly concern," and so the lesson "does not forbid contraception *per se.*"[268]

The extent of Waltke's argument for what he calls "limiting family size," though, is even more audacious. Not only does he conclude that contraception is permissible, but he spends much of the article justifying *abortion* from Scripture! For support, he asserts that, contrary to Assyrian law of the time, there is an "absence of any biblical text forbidding abortion." Surely God would have spoken more clearly if he thought this subject was important, argues Waltke. He also points out that Leviticus 24:17 calls for capital punishment of murderers, but Exodus 21:22–24 does not call for the same sentence if a preborn baby is killed in an attack. Therefore, he concludes, "God does not regard the fetus as a soul" and this suggests that "abortion was permissible" for the Israelites.[269]

Although such reasoning may sound surprising now, Waltke's views were entirely within the Evangelical mainstream at the time. There was more hesitancy about justifying abortion than contraception, to be sure, but in general, most Protestants considered both contraception and abortion to be "Catholic issues" and they didn't see a need to object to either. Indeed, just a few months before publishing this issue, *Christianity Today* had co-sponsored, along with the Christian Medical Society, a Symposium on the Control of Human Reproduction, at which they brought together thirty Evangelical scholars to hash out these issues. The conclusion, as reported by CT: not only is contraception morally acceptable, but so are most abortions. With some exceptions, the delegates "agreed that some therapeutic abortions are necessary," and "generally endorsed abortion guidelines approved in May by the American College of Obstetricians and Gynecologists."[270]

The Southern Baptist Convention echoed this view in 1971, passing a resolution at its St. Louis convention calling "Southern Baptists to work for legislation that will allow the possibility of abortion under such conditions as rape, incest, clear evidence of severe fetal deformity, and carefully ascertained evidence of the likelihood of damage to the emotional, mental, and physical health of the mother."[271] After the dreadful Roe v. Wade decision rewarded such efforts in 1973, the SBC reaffirmed its position at subsequent conferences in 1974 and 1976. W.A. Criswell, prominent pastor of First Baptist Church in Dallas and former president of the SBC, celebrated the Roe decision: "I have always felt that it was only after a child was born and had a life separate from its mother that it became an individual person and it has always, therefore, seemed to me that what is best for the mother and for the future should be allowed."[272] As Alan Carlson comments, "At the Evangelical leadership level, at least, Margaret Sanger's victory was complete."[273]

Meanwhile, the more liberal wings of American Protestantism were serving as Sanger's foot soldiers. By the late 1960s, hundreds of Protestant ministers were part of an underground network that connected women desiring abortions with doctors willing to perform them.[274] Those who had become ordained to shepherd souls to heaven were instead leading mothers and babies to physical and spiritual death.

Fifty years later, more than 63,000,000 babies have perished,[275] and abortion is seen by a large percentage of the country as an essential human right. Given the cultural power Protestantism still possessed back then, it's hard not to look back and wonder how many of those tiny lives could have been saved today if the Bible Alone crowd had not capitulated to the twisting of Scripture then.

THE CATHOLIC DIFFERENCE

On September, 21, 1957, Margaret Sanger appeared on ABC's *Mike Wallace Interview* to answer some direct questions about her life and the movement she spearheaded. It was a remarkable conversation in many ways, not least because Sanger was so clear in her disdain for traditional notions of morality, as well as the institution she saw as the premier advocate of those beliefs. When asked by Wallace to name the source of her primary opposition, she stated plainly, "The opposition is mainly from the hierarchy of the Roman Catholic Church."[276]

She was right. From the early days of her crusade, Sanger had butted heads with Catholics and the dogma of the Church. Now, that is not to say that all Catholics were following the Church's teaching. As with all the topics we have covered, many Catholics disobeyed, as Sanger herself told Wallace in that interview, explaining that Catholics were coming to her "clinics" as much as anyone else was. But the Church's refusal to officially come on board, as so many Protestant groups had done, created a constant thorn in her side.

One of Sanger's earliest public enemies was Fr. John A. Ryan. A prolific author and outspoken moral theologian, Ryan was one of the clearest prophetic voices of the early twentieth century. Writing in *Ecclesiastical Review*, Ryan predicted that marriages and society were going to suffer grave consequences if it continued down this road: "[Contraceptive] devices are debasing for those who employ them, inasmuch as they lead inevitably to loss of reverence for the marital relation, loss of respect for the conjugal partner, and loss of faith in the sacredness of the nuptial bond."[277]

Ryan also was concerned that couples using contraception exhibited a "love of material goods and a self-indulgence"[278] and he campaigned for an approach to economics that showed concern for the poor instead. Like Sanger, Ryan had grown up in a family with eleven children and knew the hardships that accompanied such an undertaking. However, rather than proposing to fix that through mechanically limiting family size, Ryan called for employers to pay just wages that would allow everyone who wanted to work hard to be able to support a family, and for employees to reject avarice. For Ryan, as well as other Catholic theologians of the time such as Fr. Ignatius Cox and Fr. John Cooper, the problem was not overpopulation, but consumerism and unjust wages.[279]

After that infamous Lambeth Conference of 1930, Catholic leaders became even more outspoken about these issues, and the Vatican quickly put together an official response. Within four months, Pope Pius XII released *Casti Connubii*, a straightforward, uncompromising encyclical that celebrated the "dignity of chaste wedlock" and condemned contraception as a "shameful and intrinsically vicious deed" that is "against nature" and for which "no reason, however grave, may be put forward" (55).

Casti Connubii also strongly condemned eugenics and called for governments of the world to protect the poor and vulnerable rather than kill them or try to keep them from being born. Referring to "the neo-paganism of today," Pius XII decried the "sad state of affairs" that accompanies the breakdown of the family and called for action to build up marriage. The encyclical reiterated the consistent Catholic position that every single person is made in the image of God and therefore has dignity; as such all are worthy of our respect and care.

That understanding of the sanctity of life is key to Catholic thought, which is based on natural truths accessible through reason as well as the authoritative interpretation of divine revelation that *sola scriptura* can never provide. As moral theologian Fr. John Ford said at the time, the Catholic answer not only to contraception and eugenics but to related issues such as sterilization, abortion, and euthanasia "is the absolute invisibility of the right of an innocent human person to life, and the absolute intrinsic evil of the act by which he is deprived of life."[280] A commitment to this principle as enduring and unshakeable by the changing fashions of biblical interpretation is why Catholics were are the forefront of each of these issues in the early twentieth century. Indeed, they often stood alone.[281]

This moral leadership continued through the forties and fifties, with Catholic bishops and priests in America paying increased attention to life issues, especially contraception. This was spurred in part, as Leslie Woodstock Tenter explains, "by a sense of crisis with regard to the health of the family."[282] The Brooklyn Diocesan Council of

Catholic Women, for example, explained it was co-sponsoring a marriage education program because "the spirit of materialism has so far infected our Catholic young women," that the ideal of Christian marriage has in some instances "been completely lost and in a great many more been alarmingly weakened." [283] The Council also noted the increase in divorce among Catholics, as well as the increase in birth control, as stark evidences of this fact. [284] Around the country, marriage preparation material included clear instruction about the Church's teaching, and parish and diocesan programs were developed to help strengthen family life. They were not always successful at keeping Catholics faithful, of course, but the teaching was clear for anyone with eyes to see and ears to hear. And it was about to get even clearer.

The Most Despised Encyclical Ever Written

One of the reasons that *Christianity Today* took such a vocal stand on contraception in the summer and fall of 1968, after essentially sitting out the discussion for most of the decade, was that in July of that year Pope Paul VI had dropped a bombshell encyclical on the topic: the highly anticipated *Humanae Vitae.*

The "Catholic 1960s," historians like to say, had begun on October 11, 1962 with the formal opening of the Second Vatican Council in Rome. [285] Originally greeted with a yawn from most Americans, as the revolutionary decade progressed and the council displayed what appeared to be a new openness to changing the Church teaching and practice, media and popular interest grew. Would the Church get on board with the rest of the world? More specifically, would it change its teaching regarding contraception?

Although contraception was not a topic for the council, it was being discussed in the Church. Pope John XXIII had established the Pontifical Commission for the Study of Population, Families and Births in 1963 and then when he died, Paul VI greatly expanded its scope and mission. By the time it produced a report in 1966, there was a general expectation that the seventy-two-member advisory committee wanted the Church to change its teaching. When the Pope announced he would release an encyclical on the topic, therefore, much of the world anticipated being able to celebrate the Church's new approval of birth control.

They were in for a shock. With *Humanae Vitae*, Paul VI instead boldly and unequivocally reaffirmed the traditional doctrines regarding sex, marriage, and contraception. He also made four predictive observations about the effects of contraception on a society: 1) It will lead to a general lowering of moral standards across the board; 2) it will lead to an increase in marital infidelity, illegitimacy, and divorce, with all their associated problems; 3) men will not treat women with the dignity they deserve, but rather objectify and use them, and women will start to see themselves as objects for men to use; and 4) governments will use contraception as a tool for authoritarian control of the population.

The outrage and dissent were immediate and widespread. Secularists and Protestants laughed at and scorned the pope, of course, but so did many within the Church. Priests, laity, and university faculties openly defied or simply ignored the document, continuing their embrace of the Sexual Revolution.

The Protestant and secular press reveled in this, taking the opportunity to attack the very notions of Church authority and papal infallibility. *Christianity Today* compared the Catholic Church to the U.S.S.R. and the pope to a communist dictator, claiming that he was flexing his authoritarian muscle over poor Catholic parishioners. In an audacious and thoroughly ignorant closing paragraph, the editors then called for dissenting Catholics to leave and find the "biblical" truth:

What are Protestants to make of the current crisis in Catholic authority? Those whose theological roots rest deep in the biblical theology of the Reformation recognize the present challenge to the papal authority that elevates church tradition over biblical teaching as a possible step toward Christian freedom and truth. They join with dissenting Catholics in their opposition to a position on birth control that exhibits a non-scriptural misunderstanding of the role of sex in marriage. And, more important, they hope that the convictions that lead Catholics to follow conscience in the matter of birth control will also guide them to a complete rejection of the false doctrine of papal infallibility and an openness to God's truth as revealed in Scripture. Freedom from the tyranny of institution and tradition could open the way to the full life of revealed truth and service. Such a life is possible for men whose source of life and authority is Jesus Christ. God's living word, revealed by the Holy Spirit through the Bible, God's written word.[286]

For its part, the *New York Times* ran a front-page story with a headline that screamed, "CATHOLIC EXPERTS IN STRONG DISSENT ON EDICT BY POPE; 87 Theologians, Mostly of Clergy, Say Birth Control Ban Is Not Binding" A secondary headline on the same page read "DECREE HELD FALLIBLE; Group of Washington Clerics Gives Support and Sees No Issue of Disloyalty"[287]

These clerics were wrong, just like those who supported slavery and Jim Crow laws. As I have mentioned throughout this book, that many Catholics, including priests, have dissented from or failed to practice what the Church teaches doesn't alter the fact that the Church teaches those things. This did not change in 1968 and it has not changed since.

Theology of the Body

Indeed, Church teaching on sexual morality has actually become fuller and more detailed, thanks in part to one of the bishops who influenced the composition *Humanae Vitae*, Karol Wojtyla—the future Pope John Paul II. Fr. Wojtyla had first started writing about these topics in the late 1950s as a professor at the Catholic University of Lublin in Poland, where he had shepherded a group of young adults through the trials and temptations of the time. He could see that the Sexual Revolution was a disaster, and he also knew that the Church had the answer. Unfortunately, many people were missing or ignoring that answer because it was often packaged merely as a rule ("Don't have premarital sex!" Don't take the Pill!") rather than including a positive philosophy of life. Wojtyla's work set out to address that problem. As Christopher West explains,

> Inadequate legalistic formulations of moral theology coupled with disparaging treatments of sexual matters by some previous churchmen had led countless people to turn a deaf ear to the Church whenever she spoke on sexual matters. John Paul II was confident, however, that he had something to say that could make a difference.[288]

In 1960, he published *Love and Responsibility*, a philosophical treatise about the nature of love, sex, and the human person. Then, when he became pope in 1978, he almost immediately commenced a series of Wednesday audiences that expanded on those themes. After 129 of these sessions, the content of these audiences was collected into what became known as the *Theology of the Body*: his effort to flesh out and unpack the depths of what Paul VI had stated succinctly in *Humanae Vitae*.

In both *Love and Responsibility* and the *Theology of the Body*, St. John Paul II sought to offer a vision of the human person that celebrated the greatness and dignity of life. God's plan for humanity (including sex) was not to restrict our freedom or dampen our enjoyment, but to give us more freedom and true happiness. The mainstream culture was teaching that the Sexual Revolution was about freedom and that traditional Christian moral teaching—which Catholicism upheld but mainstream Protestantism, thanks to *sola scriptura*, had been steadily abandoning—was a burden on freedom. John Paul knew that the truth was exactly the opposite. To see that, though, he needed to frame the issue properly and ask the right questions. As West observes:

> He believed he could demonstrate that *Humanae Vitae* was not against man but unstintingly for him; that *Humanae Vitae* was not opposed to erotic love and sexual pleasure but called men and women to the most spiritually intense experiences of them. To get there, however, questions surrounding sexual morality needed to be reframed. Instead of asking, "How far can I go before I break the law?" we need to ask, "What does it mean to be human?" "What is a person?" "What does it mean to love?" "Why did God make me male or female?" "Why did God create sex in the first place?"[289]

In answering those questions, John Paul explained that, as bearers of the image of God, we are made for *love*. But by this he did not mean, as the prevailing culture did, that we are made simply to have fluttery emotions about other people (although there is nothing wrong with such emotions in themselves). Rather, he explained, we were made to *give ourselves* for the good of others, because they too are made in the image of God. To love is to sacrifice, to put others first, to offer ourselves fully to another without thought of getting anything in return. Only when we do that will we be happy and fulfilled.

The Sexual Revolution, on the other hand, teaches that we will be happy and fulfilled when we put *ourselves* and our perceived needs first, when we *use others* for our enjoyment, when we *take* from them for our good. In this model, other people are objects that exist for our pleasure, not divine-image-bearers who exist to be loved. Indeed, in this model, *we* are objects that exist for other people's pleasure. Every person is just a sex object, and our relationships are consensual transactions of mutual use.

As Sexual Revolution pioneer Helen Gurley Brown taught in her books and on the pages of *Cosmopolitan*, women should seek to be used by men: "The fact is, if you're not a sex object, that's when you have to worry," she said in an interview with the Washington Post in 1996. "To be desired sexually, in my opinion, is about the best thing there is."[290]

The contraception debate highlighted the divide between these two philosophies of life. For Brown, contraception was good because it removed self-gift from sex, enabling people to essentially use each other as masturbation devices. You could get physical pleasure from another person without the self-gift that goes with having to sacrifice yourself taking care of both that person and the baby you could have together. For John Paul II, contraception was detestable for the same reason: because you weren't giving yourself. Therefore, it wasn't a loving act. To have "protected" sex, as it came to be called, was to withhold many parts of yourself from the other person (literally withhold semen, on the part of the man, but also withhold all the commitments that should come along with the sexual act) and use him or her as a tool for physical pleasure. Contraception changes the conjugal act into something it was never intended to be. Such a fundamental perversion of the human order can only harm everyone involved.

Humanae Vitae Vindicated

And harm everyone it has done. Every prediction in *Humanae Vitae* has come to pass, and frankly, it has been worse than Paul VI anticipated.

Regarding the lowering of general moral standards and sexual objectification of women, do we even need to offer evidence that the culture is more debased now than in 1960, and that women have been dehumanized? We are obviously worse in so many ways. Let us consider just one news item that is at the top of this father's mind as I write: the number-one song in the nation at the moment goes by the acronym WAP and includes explicit lyrics in which two female singers proudly celebrate being "whores" who let men perform sexual acts on them in exchange for money and other material things. This is the world my daughters are growing up in. They are constantly being told, in songs, movies, ads, TV shows, and Instagram feeds, that their entire identity is bound up in their body parts, and that these exist as instru ments of sexual pleasure.

Family breakdown unsurprisingly followed the trend. Adultery, illegitimacy, and divorce shot through the roof after the culture embraced the contraceptive mentality, just as Paul VI had warned. In 1960, about 5 percent of all births in America were to unmarried women; now it is about 40 percent.[291] In 1960, almost three-quarters of households were married families, but by the 2010 census it was down to less than half.[292] Cohabitation rates are now ten times higher than they were at the beginning of the sixties.[293] And although divorces have declined recently, that's only because fewer people are getting married; divorces exploded during the sixties and seventies, with divorce ending more than 50 percent of marriages by 1980. This has been devastating, especially to women and children.[294]

Regarding government control of population, it's easy to point to China's one-child policy, with its forced sterilizations and abortions, as the model example. But less-extreme cases of state-sponsored proliferation of contraception and abortion, and government intrusion into the sanctum of the family, abound all over the world.

Paul VI was right. Contraception—and the sexual chaos it empowered—has been a disaster. The Church was right all along.

Interestingly, this fact has become so obvious that even some Protestants are starting to recognize it. A small chorus of voices within Evangelicalism, particularly, has started to question Protestantism's modern pro-contraception assumptions. Southern Baptists Russell D. Moore and Al Mohler have spoken approvingly of *Humanae Vitae*, for example,[295] and the Quiverfull movement extols couples to eschew birth control and build large families. However, this is still by far the minority stance, and most Protestant leaders and scholars do not recognize the sinfulness of contraception or acknowledge its negative effects.

The Next Stage

Indeed, despite the ruins of the Sexual Revolution being all around us, many Protestants are doubling down—not only continuing to support contraception, but starting to embrace other related practices that have historically been considered grave sins. And as usual, their *sola scriptura* approach is allowing them to reinterpret Scripture to find justification.

For example, the debate over homosexuality and same-sex "marriage" in Protestantism is taking an almost identical trajectory to the debate over contraception. It is another topic on which Christianity has been almost completely united until very recently. All Christians traditionally have understood homosexual practice to be immoral, contrary to God's law, and never was the notion of same-sex matrimonial unions even entertained—until the day before yesterday—because it was considered absurd.

Without an authoritative interpreter of the Bible, however, and hopelessly committed to its private interpretation, Protestantism's walls of defense on these issues have begun breaking down, too. The more liberal mainstream denominations were the first to embrace homosexuality and same-sex unions, as we might expect, but the more conservative Evangelical groups are not far behind. And they're citing Scripture as their reason.

Evangelical author Matthew Vines, for example, made waves in 2012 when he delivered a speech to the College Hill United Methodist Church detailing his view that the Bible does not condemn homosexual behavior. Admitting that he was going against 2,000 years of interpretive tradition, Vines nevertheless stormed ahead, offering fresh takes on everything from Sodom and Gomorrah to the Sermon on the Mount.[296] The talk quickly garnered more than a million views on YouTube and led to a *New York Times* focus piece[297] and then a book deal: 2014's *God and the Gay Christian: The Biblical Case in Support of Same-Sex Relationships* quickly became a bestseller.[298]

Several Protestant theologians attempted to debunk Vines's scholarship. Albert Mohler wrote a lengthy rebuttal to the book, driven to do so "as one who must be obedient to Scripture."[299] But why must we be obedient to Mohler's interpretation over Vines's? Within a *sola scriptura* framework, there simply is no compelling reason to submit to someone else's Bible interpretation over our own—or the one that we like. The purpose statement of Vines's LGBTQ activist group, aptly named the *Reformation Project*, proclaims unironically that it is a "Bible-based" organization and promotes books with titles such as *Bible, Gender, Sexuality: Reframing the Church's Debate on Same-Sex Relationships, Transforming: The Bible and the Lives of Transgender Christians,* and *Ancient Laws and Contemporary Controversies: The Need for Inclusive Biblical Interpretation.*[300] This approach has been succeeding within Protestantism ever since the Reformation, there is no reason to think it will fail now.

Standing Firm

The Catholic Church is also sticking with what has worked, and its response to the same-sex-marriage issue has also mirrored the contraception controversy. On one hand, many Catholics are fully on board with the Sexual Revolution and embrace every new change in morality that comes down the pike. There are plenty of Catholics who support the homosexual (and now transgender) movement. On the other hand, the teaching of the Church hasn't changed. In fact, even in an age where many "progressives" think they have a pontiff who is on their side in Pope Francis, he has only reiterated the Church's traditional teaching on this subject. Indeed, in a move with echoes of the lead-up to and aftermath of *Humanae Vitae,* though many eagerly waited for him to soften Catholic teaching on homosexuality and to endorse same-sex unions, in 2021 Pope Francis approved a formal statement from the Congregation on the Doctrine of the Faith affirming that Catholic clergy cannot even give a blessing to same-sex couples. Such unions are "not ordered to the Creator's plan," the document stated, and God "does not and cannot bless sin."[301]

God cannot and does not bless sin, and the Church he founded does not and will not bless sin. However, by leaving the Church and turning to "the Bible alone," the Protestant Reformers opened the door for Christians to re-imagine a God who *does* bless sin, including in the ever-widening realm of sexual ethics. In the 500 years since Luther offered *sola scriptura* as a guiding principle for faith and morals, Protestant Christians have progressively and perversely used the Bible to justify all manner of sexual immorality in the name of God, and consequently stand at least partly to blame for the ruined lives left in their wake.

Our culture is facing a reckoning. We live in an age in which truth has perished in the streets (Isa. 59:14), and everyone is doing what is right in their own eyes (Judg. 21:25). We need God's Word to arrest the slide and enable us to turn back to him. But the Bible alone is not enough to provide it. His Church is the divinely appointed vehicle, and I encourage each of you to consider what God's role for you in it, and in its mission, might be.

SOLA SCRIPTURA AND THE WORLD'S RECKONING

The moral landscape of our culture is changing so quickly that to write about what sins Scripture will be used to justify next is to run the risk of being out of date before the book is printed. For example, the homosexuality issue we discussed at the end of the previous chapter is quickly being subsumed by transgenderism, a Satanic attack on the dignity of the human person that exploded onto the cultural landscape around 2015.[302] Since that time, thousands of young lives have been sucked into a trans-industrial complex, a cultish conglomeration of activist pharmaceutical salespeople, doctors, therapists, teachers, and parents that encourages children to take puberty blocking hormones and amputate healthy sex organs.[303] As a father, high school teacher, and documentary filmmaker who has been immersed in uncovering the horrors of this phenomenon for the past couple of years, I assure you that the reality is worse than I can adequately describe here.

Unfortunately, as always, *sola scriptura* is proving unable to withstand this cultural tsunami. Not only have many wings of Protestantism already embraced this evil—they have been justifying it with Scripture since the beginning of the movement. Indeed, by the summer of 2016, the *Washington Post* was already running an opinion piece by "bisexual Christian writer" Eliel Cruz titled, "Where in the Bible does it say you can't be transgender? Nowhere."[304] In it, Cruz follows the template that "Bible-believing" social "progressives" have been using for centuries.

For example, he starts with the argument from silence, stating, "There is not a single verse in Scripture that discusses transgender identities."[305] What about Deuteronomy 22:5, you might ask, which says, "A woman must not wear men's clothing, nor a man wear women's clothing, for the Lord your God detests anyone who does this"? That passage isn't a problem, claims Cruz, because it refers to "crossdressing," not "being trans," which is "embodying a gender that does not align with the one that was given at birth." Therefore, "to use this verse to condemn transgender identities requires ignorance of transgender identities and laziness in interpretation."[306]

Well, then, how about the creation story in Genesis? Conservative evangelicals often point to this foundational passage to argue that God created humans "male and female," not transgendered.[307] Cruz has an answer for that, too:

Genesis 1:27 says: "So God created mankind in his own image, in the image of God he created them; male and female he created them." It's this interpretation of "and" between male and female that creates a foundation for understanding gender to be binary. But the "and" isn't meant to be binary.

Genesis 1:1 says: "God created the heavens and the earth." In reading this verse, Christians interpret that God created not just the sky and the ground but everything in between. The "and" encompasses a spectrum by pointing to the two ends of the spectrum. Similarly, scripture says God is the "alpha and omega," the first and last letters of the Greek alphabet. That's not meant to say God is just those two letters. God is the entire alphabet, from alpha to omega and everything in between. As Alan Hooker and others have noted, Christians acknowledge throughout Scripture that "and" represents a spectrum, not a binary.

Cruz adds,

An anti-trans understanding of the Genesis story also lacks context. Gender and sex are different things. They don't always align, and neither is binary. The biological reality of intersex individuals is a testament to that. The biological and psychological reality of transgender and intersex individuals needs to be the context in which Christians read scripture.[308]

This exegetical theme is echoed a powerful liberal activist group called the Human Rights Campaign. In an article titled, "What Does the Bible Say About Transgender People," they exegete Genesis 1 and 2 to argue that "God's creation exists in spectrums," not binaries. So, for example, even though the Bible seems to present land and sea as binary opposites, in actuality we know that "between land and sea we have coral reefs and estuaries and beaches; between flying birds and swimming fish we have penguins and high jumping dolphins, not to mention that uncategorizable favorite the platypus!"[309] The article concludes, "No one would argue that a penguin is an abomination for not fitting the categories of Genesis 1, or that an estuary isn't pleasing to God because it's neither land nor sea. In the same way, God gives every human a self that is unique and may not always fit neatly into a box or binary."[310]

This is the type of interpretation that enables churches such as the First Congregational Church of Pasadena to put giant posters on their building declaring "God's pronouns are they/them."[311] But such advocacy is not limited to mainline liberal denominations. Mark Wingfield, former associate pastor at Wilshire Baptist Church in Dallas, offers an almost identical interpretation of the same passages for the *Baptist News* in a piece headlined "Why being transgender is not a sin."[312]

What are we to make of these arguments? Catholics can rely on authoritative Church teaching and its interpretation of Genesis 1 to reject these new explanations of the text.[313] But what about those who rely on the Bible alone? There is simply no way to definitively reject these interpretations. And that means that, once again, Protestants will be ultimately unable to resist this new cultural tidal wave.

I had a conversation with an Evangelical friend recently that I believe represents a typical *sola scriptura* approach to the issue. She is a wonderful, caring mother of teenage girls, and some friends of her daughters started identifying as trans. Dutifully, the mom started doing research and found a book on the issue—a book that presented pro-trans biblical arguments. Having no solid standard by which to judge, she began to find them persuasive and was leaning toward acceptance of the trans fad (at least until she found out about the film I was producing and we had a three-hour conversation about the topic). My friend is far from alone. Christians throughout America are struggling to deal with a shift in our culture's moral winds, and many will succumb. Transgenderism is the present and near-term future crisis, but it isn't the end. It is paving the way for mainstream acceptance and celebration of depravities such as pedophilia and transhumanism.[314] What will *sola scriptura* Christians do then?

★★★

For Protestants reading this book: I implore you to take a close, hard, look at *sola scriptura* and where it has led us. As a convert, I know just how difficult this is, but please do not let your theological habits and preconceived notions about what you believe and why keep you from an honest assessment of the Bible Alone approach to Christianity.

And for Catholics: I ask you to take an honest look at your position as well. Far too many Catholics today ignore the Church's teaching in many areas, from consumerism to contraception. This is a terrible witness to the world. In Romans 2:17-24, Paul slammed the religious leaders of his day who lived contrary to the faith they professed to follow: "God's name is blasphemed among the Gentiles because of you." Cafeteria Catholics who pick and choose what doctrines they accept while living immoral lives are doing the same. On the other hand, let us be encouraged by those Catholics who live out the Faith in the midst of much opposition and scorn, as well as those brave Church leaders and pastors who are unashamed of the Church's authoritative interpretation of divine revelation and who are willing to use the authority vested in them to keep the rest of us on track.[315]

Our culture is facing a reckoning. We need God's Word to arrest the slide and enable us to turn back to him. But the Bible alone is not enough to provide it. His Church is the divinely appointed vehicle, and I encourage each of you to consider what God's role for you in it, and in its mission, might be.

ABOUT THE AUTHOR

Donald J. Johnson is a filmmaker, speaker, and radio show host. As the founder and president of Runaway Planet Pictures and Don Johnson Media, Don's projects include the documentaries *Unprotected*, *Convinced*, and *Dysconnected*, as well as the book *How to Talk to a Skeptic*. To learn more, please visit donjohnsonmedia.com.

ENDNOTES

---

1   There is no shortage of scandal to cite, but to offer just one example, as I write this, the biggest story in American Christianity is a report on the double life of Ravi Zacharias. A world-renowned evangelist who died in 2020, Zacharias was also a serial abuser of women. See more at https://www.christianitytoday.com/news/2021/february/ravi-zacharias-rzim-investigation-sexual-abuse-sexting-rape.html .

2   For a fuller discussion of the poll data, see Ronald J. Sider, *The Scandal of the Evangelical Conscience* (Grand Rapids: Baker, 2005).

3   Sider, 17.

4   C.S. Lewis makes this case eloquently in *Mere Christianity* (New York, Macmillan, 1960).

5   Even as religion is often charged with being the cause of political violence, it is actually atheistic regimes that have produced the most deadly authoritarian violence. For a discussion, see https://www.wordonfire.org/resources/blog/is-religion-responsible-for-the-worlds-violence/19917/.

6   My study eventually led me into the Catholic Church. I view my conversion not as a rejection of Protestantism or my upbringing, but as the continuation and fulfillment of my upbringing. I didn't lose anything in becoming Catholic (other than a few friends and a lot of income); I simply gained. For example, not only do I now have the authority of the Magisterium to help guide me with Scripture, but I also have the sacraments, the saints, and so much more.

7   *Forensic justification* is the "declaration that believers are righteous rather than the process by which they are *made* righteous, involving a change in their *status* rather than in their *nature*" (Alistair McGrath, *Iustitia Dei: A History of the Doctrine of Justification*, New York: Cambridge University Press, 2005, 212. Italics in original). As the Protestant McGrath readily admits, this doctrine was a "theological novelty" at the time of the Reformation. In other words, it was a new belief that had never been held previously in the history of the Church. He writes, "The most accurate description of the doctrines of justification associated with the Reformed and Lutheran churches from 1530 onward is that they represent a radically new interpretation of the Pauline concept of 'imputed righteousness'" (209).

   Defenders of forensic justification sometimes assert that the Reformers simply rediscovered the beliefs of the early Church (or at least Augustine), but Francis Beckwith argues that a full-blown doctrine of forensic justification was simply not held prior to the Reformation. "One does not find it in the ante-Nicene, Nicene, or post-Nicene Fathers. One does not find it in the Latin or Eastern rites of the Church" (Francis J. Beckwith, *Return to Rome: Confessions of an Evangelical Catholic*. Grand Rapids: Brazos Press, 2009, 112.) It simply didn't exist.

8   Louis Bouyer puts it like this: "It is certain that the process of [Luther's] thought . . . did not by any means originate in some general theory on authority in matters of faith and lead up to a particular conclusion about authority. On the contrary, it was a living intuition of salvation that crystallized his view of the Bible (*The Spirit and Forms of Protestantism*, Princeton: Scepter Press, 1956, 143).

145

9   Brad S. Gregory *The Unintended Reformation: How a Religious Revolution Secularized Society* (Cambridge: Harvard University Press, 2012), 89.

10 Gregory, 89.

11 Ibid., 90.

12 Gregory, 98.

13 Preserved Smith, *The Life and Letters of Martin Luther*, Boston and New York: Houghton Mifflin Company, 1911, 291-292; letter from Wittenberg, February or beginning of March, 1532, quoted in Dave Armstrong, "Luther on the Deaths of Zwingli, St. Thomas More, & St. John Fisher," https://www.patheos.com/blogs/davearmstrong/2017/10/luther-deaths-zwingli-st-thomas-st-john-fisher.html.

14 O'Hare, Patrick F., *The Facts About Luther*, 214. Kindle Edition.

15 Desiderius Erasmus, *De libero arbitrio diatribe, sive collatio* (Basel: Johannes Froben, 1524), sig. b1. quoted in Gregory, 99.

16 Ibid.

17 Regula Bochsler, "The Anabaptist Felix Manz meets a terrible end," available at https://www.swissinfo.ch/eng/the-reformation-eats-its-young_the-anabaptist-felix-manz-meets-a-terrible-end/43485650.

18 The term *Radical Reformers* generally connotes those Protestants who rebelled against "magisterial" Protestant leaders such as Luther and Calvin, but this is a bit of a misnomer. There really was no essential difference between the two groups; they all held to *sola scriptura* and in so doing followed their own differing interpretations. Luther and Calvin, however, had political power to enforce their beliefs on others (contrary to the teaching of *sola scriptura* of course), whereas Anabaptists and other smaller Protestant groups did not. Lutheranism and Calvinism gained more followers and eventually took on more of a "traditional" nature and structure only because they gained the backing of states early in their history. See more on this in Gregory.

19 Noll, Mark *God and Mammon: Protestants, Money, and the Market, 1790-1860* (New York: Oxford University Press, 2002), 4.

20 See https://twitter.com/grcastleberry/status/1230928705159147525.

21 Christie Storm "Tabling the altar: Its purpose and presence have been altered over time," *Arkansas Democrat Gazette*, January 30, 2010, available at https://www.arkansasonline.com/news/2010/jan/30/tabling-altar-20100130/.

22 I realize that Protestants try to offer a bunch of other reasons to attend, but you don't have to look any further than the mega-churches in the country to realize that the characteristic they all share is a talented preacher. People go where they like the message, and no matter how many other programs you offer, if people don't like the preaching, the enterprise will shrink.

23 O'Hare, 215.

24 George O'Brien, *The Economic Effects of the Reformation* (Norfolk, VA, IHS Press, 2003), 50.

25 Obrien, 51.

26 Ibid.

27 Ibid.

28 Steve Weidenkopf, "Did the Church Ever Support Slavery?", available at https://www.catholic.com/magazine/online-edition/did-the-church-ever-support-slavery.

29 This view was built on works such as Gomes Eanes de Zurara's influential 1453 book *The Chronicle of the Discovery and Conquest of Guinea*, which defends the Portuguese slave trade by describing Africans as savage animals who were better off being slaves

in the West: "They lived like beasts without any custom of reasonable things . . . they have no knowledge of bread and wine, and they were without covering of clothes, or the lodgment of houses, and worse than all they had no understanding of good, but only knew how to live in bestial sloth" (Gomes Eanes de Zurara, *The Chronicle of the Discovery and Conquest of Guinea*, 2 vols. (London: Printed for the Hakluyt Society, 1896), 29). Fourteenth-century philosopher and slave trade supporter Ibn Khaldun echoed this notion: "The Negro nations are, as a rule, submissive to slavery because they have little that is (essentially) human and possess attributes that are quite similar to dumb animals" (Gomes Eanes de Zurara, *The Chronicle of the Discovery and Conquest of Guinea*, 2 vols. (London: Printed for the Hakluyt Society, 1896), 29).

30 Ibn Khaldun, Franz Rosenthal, and N.J. Dawood, *The Muqaddimah: An Introduction to History*, Bollingen Series (Princeton, NJ: Princeton University Press, 1969), 11.

31 Gary Taylor, *Buying Whiteness: Race, Culture, and Identify from Columbus to Hip-hop* (New York: Palgrave Macmillan, 2005), 229.

32 Cotton Mather, *The Negro Christianized: An essay to excite and assist the good work, the instruction of Negro-servants in Christianity:* Early English Books Online Text Creative Partnership, 2011. https://quod.lib.umich.edu/e/evans/N01059.0001.001/1:2?rgn=di v1;view=fulltext Accessed 11-24-2021

33 Ibid.

34 Paul Bayne, *An Entire Commentary upon the Whole Epistle of St. Paul to the Ephesians* (Princeton, NJ: Princeton University Press) available at http://www.digitalpuritan. net/Digital%20Puritan%20Resources/Baynes,%20Paul/Commentary%20on%20 Ephesians.pdf.

35 Mather, https://quod.lib.umich.edu/e/evans/N01059.0001.001/1:2?rgn=div1;view=f ulltext, accessed 11-24-2021.

36 Mather, *The Negro Christianized* https://digitalcommons.unl.edu/ zeaamericanstudies/5/.

37 Tisby, Jemar, *The Color of Compromise* (38). Zondervan. Kindle Edition.

38 Tisby, 25.

39 Emerson and Smith, 24.

40 Haynes, Stephen R., *Noah's Curse: The Biblical Justification of American Slavery* (Oxford: Oxford University Press, 2002), Kindle Locations 1066-1068.

41 George Armstrong, *The Christian Doctrine of Slavery* (New York: Charles Scribner, 1857) https://static1.squarespace.com/static/590be125ff7c502a07752a5b/t/59e5dc9f3 7c58193140b510c/1506139307268/Armstrong%2C+George+D.+-1The+Christian+ Doctrine1 of+Slavery.pdf, accessed November 24, 2021.

42 Ibid.

43 Haynes, Kindle locations 1566-1569.

44 Henry J. Van Dyke, "The Character and Influence of Abolitionism," in *Fast Day Sermons; or, The Pulpit on the State of the Country* (New York: Rudd and Carleton, 1861), 139.

45 Mark A. Noll, *The Civil War as a Theological Crisis* (The Steven and Janice Brose Lectures in the Civil War Era), 39. The University of North Carolina Press. Kindle Edition.

46 Paul A. Johnson, *A History of Christianity* (New York: Touchstone, 1976), 438.

47 Ibid.

48 Noll, 4.

49 Johnson, 438.

50 Benjamin Morgan, Thanksgiving Sermon, November 29, 1860. https:// civilwarcauses.org/palmer.htm, accessed November 24, 2021.

51 Cannon, 89.

52 Haynes, Kindle Locations 2029–2030.

53 Ibid., Kindle Locations 2037–2039.

54 Widespread segregation in the form of white-only churches or seated sections and other forms of second-class membership for blacks was a big reason behind the formation of what we now call "historically black" churches. See C. Eric Lincoln and Lawrence Mamirya, *The Black Church in the African American Experience* (Durham, NC: Duke University Press, 1990), 27.

55 Rev. G.T. Gillespie, *A Christian View on Segregation* speech made before the Synod of Mississippi of the Presbyterian Church, November 4, 1954. Available at https://egrove.olemiss.edu/citizens_pamph/1/?utm_source=egrove. olemiss.edu%2Fcitizens_pamph%2F1&utm_medium=PDF&utm_ campaign=PDFCoverPages, accessed November 24, 2021.

56 Cannon, 94.

57 Haynes, Kindle locations 1313-1319.

58 Gerencser, Bruce, "Is Segregation Scriptural? by Evangelist Bob Jones Sr., the Founder of Bob Jones University." Available at https://brucegerencser.net/2017/08/is-segregation-scriptural-by-evangelist-bob-jones-the-founder-of-bob-jones-university.

59 "Bob Jones University Drops Interracial Dating Ban," available at https://www. christianitytoday.com/ct/2000/marchweb-only/53.0.html.

60 "The Preacher who used Christianity to revive the Ku Klux Klan," DeNeen L. Brown, *Washington Post*, April 10, 2018. https://www.washingtonpost.com/news/ retropolis/wp/2018/04/08/the-preacher-who-used-christianity-to-revive-the-ku-klux-klan/.

61 Juan O. Sanchez, *Religion and the Ku Klux Klan: Biblical Appropriation in Their Literature and Songs* (Jefferson, NC: McFarland, 2016), 14.

62 J.B. Kelly, *The Gospel According to the Klan* (CultureAmerica) (39-40). University Press of Kansas. Kindle Edition.

63 Ibid., 43.

64 W.C. Wright, "The Twelfth Chapter of Romans as a Klansman's Law of Life," from John Martin Smith Ku Klux collection at the Eckhart Public Library's Online Photo Archive, https://willennar.pastperfectonline.com/library/5F091C67-CF89-47BF-8E1B-498742937736, accessed November 25, 2021.

65 Kenneth T. Jackson, *The Ku Klux Klan in the City, 1915–1930* (New York: Oxford University Press, 1967), xv.

66 Adam Gussow, *Seems Like Murder Here: Southern Violence and the Blues Tradition* (Chicago: University of Chicago Press, 2002), 49.

67 Donald L. Grant, *The Anti-Lynching Movement: 1883–1932*. San Francisco: R & E Research Associates; 1975, 87.

68 Emerson and Smith, 46.

69 In his famous *Letter from a Birmingham Jail,* King confessed that he had believed that "the white ministers, priests, and rabbis of the South would be among our strongest allies." But instead, he said, "some have been outright opponents, refusing to understand the freedom movement and misrepresenting its leaders; all too many others have been more cautious than courageous and have remained silent behind the anesthetizing security of stained-glass windows."

70 Martin Luther King Jr., "I Have a Dream" speech, delivered August 28, 1963 on the steps of the Lincoln Memorial, Washington D.C. Available at https://www.npr. org/2010/01/18/122701268/i-have-a-dream-speech-in-its-entirety.

71 William Martin, *A Prophet with Honor: The Billy Graham Story* (New York: W. Morrow and Co., 1991), 296.

72 Martin, 297.

73 Richard Rothstein. *The Color of Law: A Forgotten History of How Our Government Segregated America*, Kindle Edition, 10.

74 https://www.thecatholicthing.org/2011/04/20/catholics-and-the-civil-war/.

75 Mark Summers, "Onward catholic soldiers: The Catholic Church during the American civil war," https://www.acton.org/onward-catholic-soldiers-catholic-church-during-american-civil-war.

76 For a good analysis of this issues see Mark Brumley, "Let My People Go: The Catholic Church and Slavery." https://www.catholiceducation.org/en/controversy/common-misconceptions/let-my-people-go-the-catholic-church-and-slavery.html.

He notes, among other points, that prior to the twentieth century, Catholics were a small, despised minority whose leadership was not in a position to lead a major social crusade. Other scholars, including John McGreevy and Mark Noll, have also documented the anti-Catholic spirit of antebellum America. One of the reasons some Catholics felt they couldn't work more closely with the abolitionist movement in the North, for example, was that the abolitionists viewed Catholics as on the same moral plane as slaveholders. The northern Protestant abolitionists saw both southern Evangelicals and Catholics as anti-Bible and therefore anti-Christ. For more, see McGreedy, *Catholicism and American Freedom*, and Noll, *The Civil War as Theological Crisis*.

77 This applies whether the offending party is a clergy or a layperson. A good example of this principle in action occurred at the 1855 meeting of the Massachusetts Anti-Slavery Society. According to the minutes, Henry Kemp responded to an anti-Catholic comment by explaining that the Catholic Church had officially condemned slavery and that all the faithful should put it entirely away from them in the name of Almighty God.

78 Pastoral letter of Archbishop Rummel, March 15, 1953, available at https://archives. arch-no.org/ckeditor_assets/attachments/194/blessedarethepeacemakers.pdf, quoted in Brian Harper, "There's no segregation in the kingdom of heaven," https://www. ncronline.org/news/opinion/young-voices/theres-no-segregation-kingdom heaven

79 John Smestad Jr. "The Role of Archbishop Joseph F. Rummel in the Desegregation of Catholic Schools in New Orleans," http://people.loyno.edu/~history/journal/1993-4/Smestad.html.

80 Ibid.

81 MacGregor, Morris J. *Steadfast in the Faith: The Life of Patrick Cardinal Boyle* (Washington, D.C.: Catholic University of America Press, 2006), 195-196.

82 Tim O'Neil, "Parents Protest after St. Louis Catholic Schools are integrated" *St. Louis Post-Dispatch*, https://www.stltoday.com/news/archives/sept-parents-protest-after-st-louis-catholic-schools-are-integrated/article_fed00718-1449-56ff-9c31-50115a468059.html#6.

83 The details on what constitutes "similar enough" vary among churches and denominations, of course, and the degree to which churches make a big deal out of their beliefs varies as well. Some churches are adamant that you must believe Calvin on predestination, others that you have to believe in a literal thousand-year reign of

Christ, and so on. Most, though, are fairly wishy-washy on everything these days. They are more concerned just that you attend.

84 The names of the shoppers on this page are pseudonyms.

85 https://www.budgetsaresexy.com/financial-confessional-amazon-shopaholic/.

86 https://www.refinery29.com/en-ca/covid19-shopping-addiction-experiences.

87 https://www.dailymail.co.uk/health/article-7686329/Online-shopping-addiction-mental-health-condition-officially-recognised.html.

88 https://money.com/online-shopping-late-night-impulse-buy-stress/.

89 https://www.huffpost.com/entry/unworn-clothing-survey_n_5048486.

90 https://www.fool.com/investing/2020/12/30/if-youre-retired-consider-buying-these-3-stocks-in/.

91 http://www.weardonaterecycle.org.

92 https://www.theatlantic.com/business/archive/2014/07/where-does-discarded-clothing-go/374613/.

93 https://slate.com/human-interest/2012/06/the-salvation-army-and-goodwill-inside-the-places-your-clothes-go-when-you-donate-them.html. The clothes that can't be sold at thrift stores have historically been shipped to poor countries overseas, but even that market is drying up as textile manufacturing becomes even cheaper. See https://appareinsider.com/nowhere-to-go-for-used-clothing-as-markets-dry-up/.

94 James B. Twitchell, "Two Cheers for Materialism," *The Wilson Quarterly (1976-)*, vol. 23, no. 2, 1999, 16–26. *JSTOR*, www.jstor.org/stable/40259880, accessed December 30, 2020.

95 Gregory, 236.

96 https://www.nytimes.com/2021/01/04/business/china-covid19-freedom.html. The article goes so far as to extol the virtues of *China* as a model of the freedom we should desire in a post-pandemic world, because it was the fastest to return to having all the best consumeristic qualities—packed hotels and restaurants, lines at luxury stores—of pre-pandemic America.

97 Twitchell.

98 See the 28-minute mark of "Ford and the American Dream" by Lorin Sorenson at https://www.youtube.com/watch?v=ZrOikS5B2gs.

99 See Gregory, 237 and Zygmunt Bauman, *Does Ethics Have a Chance in a World of Consumers* (Cambridge, Mass. and London: Harvard University Press, 2008), 42-55, 157-172.

100 https://medium.com/@erikrittenberry/the-american-life-is-killing-you-9e7e68135f4a.

101 St. Augustine, *Confessions* (Lib 1 ,1-2, 2.5, 5: CSEL 33, 1-5).

102 See chapter 4, "Love and the Meaning of Life" in Don Johnson, *How to Talk to a Skeptic* (Bloomington, MN: Bethany House, 2013).

103 Herbert Schlossberg, *Idols for Destruction* (Nashville: Thomas Nelson, 1983), 88-89.

104 I owe much in this section to Randy Alcorn. His book *Money, Possessions, and Eternity* has an excellent section titled "10 Ways Materialism Brings us to Ruin," which shows how it fosters immorality and the deterioration of the family. Randy Alcorn, *Money, Possessions, and Eternity* (Carol Stream, IL: Tyndale, 2003), 53.

105 Schlossberg, 311.

106 G.K. Chesterton, *Orthodoxy* (Chicago: Moody, 2009), 178.

107 Dorothy Sayers, *Letters to a Diminished Church*. Thomas Nelson. Kindle Edition, location 987-1012.

108 Gregory, 245.

109 Sayers, location 1047

110 https://www.forbes.com/sites/forbesagencycouncil/2017/08/25/finding-brand-success-in-the-digital-world/?sh=54252cd8626e.

111 Ross Douthat, *Bad Religion: How We Became a Nation of Heretics* (New York: Free Press, 2012), 189-190.

112 See https://www.cnbc.com/2019/11/22/inside-home-depots-efforts-to-stop-a-growing-theft-problem.html. https://www.nytimes.com/2021/01/06/nyregion/car-thefts-nyc.html. https://www.shrm.org/resourcesandtools/hr-topics/employee-relations/pages/workplace-theft-on-the-rise-.aspx.

113 Some other reasons could include the mainstreaming of masking and aversion to confrontation during the COVID pandemic, the increasing ease by which stolen goods can be sold online, and a growing trend of indulgent toleration of petty crime in some municipalities.

114 https://www.theguardian.com/commentisfree/2006/jun/29/comment.ukcrime.

115 https://www.webmd.com/baby/features/rite-of-passage-cry-for-help.

116 https://www.cnbc.com/2020/05/05/consumer-debt-hits-new-record-of-14point3-trillion.html.

117 https://www.nerdwallet.com/blog/average-credit-card-debt-household/.

118 As the American Bar Association explains, "Payday lenders offer small, short-term loans (often two weeks or less) using a check dated in the future as collateral. Most borrowers cannot repay the full loan by their next payday, so they are forced to renew the loan repeatedly for additional two-week terms, paying new fees with each renewal. Ninety-nine percent of payday loans go to repeat borrowers. Over five million American families are caught in a cycle of payday debt each year, paying $3.4 billion in excess fees." https://www.americanbar.org/groups/crsj/publications/human_rights_magazine_home/human_rights_vol32_2005/summer2005/hr_summer05_predator/.

119 See, for example, Exodus 22:25. Psalm 15:5, Ezekiel 18:13, Deuteronomy 23:19-20. Also, see articles by Christopher Kaczor and David J. Palm at catholic.com for a good summary of Church teaching and the question of whether the Catholic Church has changed its position on this topic. https://www.catholic.com/magazine/print-edition/did-the-church-change-its-stance-on-usury; https://www.catholic.com/magazine/print-edition/the-red-herring-of-usury.

120 https://www.firstthings.com/web-exclusives/2009/06/dorothy-sayers-and-economic-so. The problems with relying on money making money as a way to get something for nothing (rather than actually producing something with objective value) go well beyond usury. For a good breakdown of the moral issues associated with various monetary systems, see Schlossberg, 88-139.

121 https://www.nbcnews.com/business/economy/there-are-more-payday-lenders-u-s-mcdonalds-n255156.

122 And though we may be inclined to denigrate the owners of the local Cash Stop as greedy predators, the fact is that Americans in general celebrate people who make that kind of quick, easy money. We consider the hedge fund managers who make billions overnight without producing anything as being "successful" while viewing hourly laborers as lower class. Indeed, on the day that I write this, one of the big news stories of the day is the stock market performance of GameStop, a floundering retail company whose stock has nonetheless spiked in value in the last two days because of speculators looking to make a quick fortune before it inevitably crashes. Interestingly, this bubble was created by people mad at hedge fund managers for

"shorting" GameStop, or trying to make money off its demise. https://www.cnbc.com/2021/01/27/gamestop-jumps-another-50percent-even-as-hedge-funds-cover-short-bets-scrutiny-of-rally-intensifies.html.

123 https://www.theguardian.com/global-development/2019/dec/16/apple-and-google-named-in-us-lawsuit-over-congolese-child-cobalt-mining-deaths.

124 According to the U.S. Department of Labor, "The People's Republic of China has arbitrarily detained more than one million Uyghurs and other mostly Muslim minorities in China's far western Xinjiang Uyghur Autonomous Region. It is estimated that 100,000 Uyghurs and other ethnic minority ex-detainees in China may be working in conditions of forced labor following detention in re-education camps. See the report here: https://www.dol.gov/agencies/ilab/against-their-will-the-situation-in-xinjiang.

Also, these stories: https://www.buzzfeednews.com/article/alison_killing/xinjiang-camps-china-factories-forced-labor; https://www.washingtonpost.com/technology/2020/12/29/lens-technology-apple-uighur/.

125 https://www.reuters.com/article/india-wistron-workers/violence-at-apple-supplier-in-india-fuels-fears-of-further-worker-unrest-idusl4n2iv1df.

126 https://www.thestar.com/news/2007/12/08/pope_denounces_consumerism.html.

127 https://www.businessinsider.com/pope-denounces-throwaway-culture-of-consumer-society-2015-7.

128 https://www.ncronline.org/news/parish/cantu-and-cupich-families-are-more-groups-consumers.

129 Gregory, 253-254.

130 John Colet, *Oratio habita a D. Donne Colet Decano Sancti Pauli ad Clerum in Conuocatione*, quoted in Gregory, 254.

131 Gregory, 265.

132 George O'Brien, *An Essay on The Economic Effects of the Reformation* (Norfolk, VA: IHS Press, 2003), 48.

133 For a good overview, see Brad Gregory, *The Unintended Reformation: How a Religious Revolution Secularized Society* (Cambridge, MA, Harvard University Press, 2012). Regarding money issues specifically, see chapter 5: Manufacturing the Goods Life. Also, see George O'Brien, *An Essay on The Economic Effects of the Reformation* (Norfolk, VA: IHS Press, 2003) and Amintore Fanfani, *Catholicism, Protestantism, and Capitalism* (Norfolk, VA, IHS Press, 2003).

134 Charles-Louis de Seconat, Baron de Montesquieu, *The Spirit of the Laws* (1748).

135 Gregory, 285.

136 O'Brien, 49.

137 O'Brien, 53.

138 Ralph Waldo Emerson, *English Traits*, quoted in O'Brien, 98.

139 O'Brien, 55.

140 Eugene McCarraher, *The Enchantments of Mammon: How Capitalism Became the Religion of Modernity* (The Belknap Press of Harvard University Press: Cambridge, MA, 2019), 55.

141 One way this played out was in the taking-over of charity by the state and the passing of "poor laws" that put strict limits on who could receive aid from the government. See O'Brien, 54-55.

142 Gregory, 291. Tocqueville adds,"One usually finds that love of money is either the chief or a secondary motive at the bottom of everything the Americans do. It gives a family likeness to all their passions and soon makes them wearisome to contemplate."

143 Tocqueville, *Democracy in America*, Volume I and II (Optimized for Kindle), 372. Kindle Edition.

144 For example, see https://www.whdl.org/sites/default/files/publications/EN_John_Wesley_126_on_danger_of_increasing_riches.htm.

145 David Hempton, "A Tale of Preachers and Beggars: Methodism and Money in the Great Age of Transatlantic Expansion, 1780-1830" in Mark Noll, *God and Mammon: Protestants, Money, and the Market, 1790-1860* (New York: Oxford University Press, 2002), 124.

146 "Among the strangest of the rumors circulating about early Methodism was the charge that it promoted the notion of Christian communism—'the community of goods.' In the early summer of 1739, Lord Egmont, one of the Georgia Trustees, got wind of the story and after hearing Whitefield preach at Blackheath pressed him whether, among other eccentricities, he held that 'all things should be in common.' The same year two anti-Methodist pamphlets raised the same issue, and in 1740 it surfaced again in the papers when another former Oxford Methodist, Benjamin Ingham, was accused by his local vicar of helping to foment a violent riot of Dewsbury cloth workers by 'preaching up a community of goods, as was practiced by the Primitive Christians.' Ingham was said to urge a sharing of wealth so drastic that his brother had remarked in disgust, 'If I mind our Ben, he would preach me out of all I have.'" Walsh, J. (1990). *John Wesley and the Community of Goods*. Studies in Church History. Subsidia, 7, 25-50. doi:10.1017/S0143045900001320.

147 Richard W. Pointer, "Philadelphia Presbyterians, Capitalism, and the Morality of Economic Success" in Noll, *God and Mammon*, 171.

148 Ibid., 171.

149 Ibid., 176.

150 Ibid., 182.

151 George M. Marsden, *The Evangelical Mind and the New School Presbyterian Experience* (New Haven, Conn.: Yale University Press, 1970), quoted in Ibid., 172

152 Mark A. Noll, "Protestant Reasoning About Money and the Economy, 1790-1860: A Preliminary Probe" in Noll, *God and Mammon*, 272.

153 Ibid., 272.

154 Mark Summers, "Onward Catholic Soldiers: The Catholic Church during the American Civil War" https://www.acton.org/onward-catholic-soldiers-catholic-church-during-american-civil-war.

155 Mark A. Noll, *The Civil War as a Theological Crisis* (The Steven and Janice Brose Lectures in the Civil War Era), 126. The University of North Carolina Press. Kindle Edition.

156 Summers, "Onward Catholic Soldiers."

157 Joel Osteen, *Your Best Life Now: 7 Steps to Living at Your Full Potential* (New York: Time Warner, 2004), 5.

158 https://www.theatlantic.com/magazine/archive/2009/12/did-christianity-cause-the-crash/307764/.

159 https://www.businesswire.com/news/home/20200317005829/en/The-Najafi-Companies-and-Trinity-Broadcasting-Network-TBN-Align-to-Offer-to-Acquire-Tegna-Inc.

160 https://www.theatlantic.com/magazine/archive/2009/12/did-christianity-cause-the-crash/307764/.

161 Kate Bowker, *Blessed*, 5-6. Oxford University Press. Kindle Edition.

162 Ibid.

163 Bowler, 4.

164 Douthat, 190.

165 Douthat, 186.

166 See, for example, https://www.hopefaithprayer.com/salvationnew/raised-with-him-kenyon/.

167 Bowler, 20.

168 Ibid., 45.

169 Ibid., 46.

170 Ibid., 49.

171 Kenneth Copeland, *Laws of Prosperity* (Harrison House Publishing, Tulsa, OK, 1974), 26-27.

172 Bowler, 66.

173 Ibid., 54.

174 http://voiceofhealing.info/04_other%20ministries/allen.html See also Bowler, 53, and https://en.wikipedia.org/wiki/A._A._Allen.

175 Bowler, 54.

176 http://tulsaworld.com/app/oralroberts/timeline.html; https://tulsaworld.com/archives/oral-roberts-declares-ministry-will-continue/article_eb497f2b-bb9e-5c0b-8c8a-476157078559.html.

177 Bowler, 74.

178 Peter Horsefield, Religious Television: The American Experience (New York: Longman, 1984), 88-100.

179 Bowler, 95.

180 Kenneth Hagin, *Biblical Keys to Financial Prosperity* (Broken Arrow: Rhema, 1973), 17.

181 Dreflo Dollar, *Total Life Prosperity: 14 Practical Steps to Receiving God's Full Blessing* (Nashville: Thomas Nelson, 1999), 15.

182 https://www.cnn.com/2009/LIVING/wayoflife/12/25/RichJesus/index.html.

183 Ibid.

184 Ron Sider, *Rich Christians in an Age of Hunger* is a well-known work in this area. A sixth edition was released by Thomas Nelson in 2015.

185 A simple online search will reveal any number of books, videos, and columns from Protestants slamming the prosperity gospel. In this *Huffington Post* piece, a Protestant preacher calls out Osteen and Meyer by name: https://www.huffpost.com/entry/osteen-meyer-prosperity-gospel_b_3790384.

186 https://www.youtube.com/watch?v=jLRue4nwJaA.

187 For an example, see here: https://www.youtube.com/watch?v=nO4FHUL39QQ.

188 Joel Osteen, *Hope for Today Bible* (Brentwood, TN: Howard Books, 2009).

189 https://www.theatlantic.com/magazine/archive/2009/12/did-christianity-cause-the-crash/307764/.

190 Carolyn Tuft and Bill Smith, "From Fenton to Fortune in the Name of God," *St. Louis Post-Dispatch*, November 15, 2003, quoted in Douthat, 188.

191 Ibid. Quoted here: https://rachelchitra.wordpress.com/2008/08/07/from-fenton-to-fortune-in-the-name-of-god/.

192 Michelle Lesley links at least fifteen articles apposing Joyce Meyer within the context of her own piece calling Meyer a false prophet here: https://michellelesley.com/tag/joyce-meyer-false-prophet/.

193 For an Evangelical example of a rebuttal to the prosperity preachers, see https://www.gotquestions.org/was-Jesus-rich.html. There are many arguments against Jesus' family being wealthy, but the strongest might be that Mary and Joseph presented

doves as a sacrifice at the presentation of Jesus (Luke 2:24), which was only allowable for poor families. For those that could afford it, the sacrifice was to be a lamb (Lev. 12:6-8). It seems that, at most, Jesus' family might have been what we would call working class. For more, see https://www.catholic.com/qa/was-jesus-wealthy.

194 https://www.catholicculture.org/culture/library/view.cfm?recnum=4388.

195 Ibid.

196 Ibid.

197 Ibid.

198 For an informative and well-balanced article on the Catholic position on poverty, see "Poverty," *The Catholic Encyclopedia,* available at https://www.catholic.com/encyclopedia/poverty.

199 Mary Eberstadt, *Adam and Eve After the Pill* (Kindle Locations 52-53). Ignatius Press. Kindle Edition.

200 Russell Shorto, "Contra Contraception" *New York Times Magazine,* May 7, 2006.

201 From my personal documentary interview with Jennifer Fulwiler, sections of which are available at "Jennifer Fulwiler Conversion Story," https://vimeo.com/329920522. See also Jennifer Fulwiler, *Something Other Than God* (San Francisco: Ignatius Press, 2014) as well as my films *Convinced* and *Unprotected,* available on Formed, Vimeo, and elsewhere.

202 St. Clement of Alexandria wrote, "Because of its divine institution for the propagation of man, the seed is not to be vainly ejaculated, nor is it to be damaged, nor is it to be wasted" (*The Instructor of Children* 2:10:91:2 [A.D. 191]). Also, "To have coitus other than to procreate children is to do injury to nature" (ibid., 2:10:95:3).

203 "I am supposing, then, although you are not lying [with your wife] for the sake of procreating offspring, you are not for the sake of lust obstructing their procreation by an evil prayer or an evil deed. Those who do this, although they are called husband and wife, are not; nor do they retain any reality of marriage, but with a respectable name cover a shame. Sometimes this lustful cruelty, or cruel lust, comes to this, that they even procure poisons of sterility . . . Assuredly if both husband and wife are like this, they are not married, and if they were like this from the beginning they come together not joined in matrimony but in seduction. If both are not like this, I dare to say that either the wife is in a fashion the harlot of her husband or he is an adulterer with his own wife" (*Marriage and Concupiscence* 1:15:17 [A.D. 419]).

204 St. Augustine, *On Genesis According to the Letter,* 9.7, CSEL 28: 276; quoted in Carlson, 12.

205 Martin Luther, *Luther's Works, Vol 5: Lectures on Genesis,* Chapters 1–5 (St. Louis, MO: Concordia, 1958), 117–18.

206 John Calvin, *Commentary on Genesis,* vol. I, part 4, trans. John King [1847], 5–6. quoted in Allan C. Carlson, *Godly Seed,* 42. Taylor and Francis. Kindle Edition.

207 Ibid.

208 Cotton Mather, *The Pure Nazirite.* Available at https://wellcomecollection.org/works/p8rk2qge.

209 John Wesley, *Commentary on Genesis.* Available at http://bible.christiansunite.com/wes/wes01.shtml.

210 Quoted in Mary Alden Hopkins, "Birth Control and Public Morals," *Harper's Weekly,* 60 (May 22, 1915): 490.

211 *New York Times* March 8, 1873, 7, col. 2.

212 Carlson, 48.

213 *State Papers as Governor and President*, in Works XVII quoted by Christopher West http://corproject.com/195-astonishing-things-freud-teddy-roosevelt-gandhi-and-t-s-eliot-said-about-contraception/.

214 https://www.theodorerooseveltcenter.org/Blog/Item/Sanger.

215 John T. Noonan, *Contraception: A History of Its Treatment*, by the Catholic Theologians and Canonists (Cambridge, MA: The Belknap Press of Harvard University Press, 1986), 412.

216 That was the assessment of historian James Reed, quoted in Carlson, 42.

217 Studies show that as many as two-thirds of teen girls have been asked to send nude photos of themselves, and my experience with families of school-age children confirms this. It is one of our biggest struggles as parents right now. See https://www.psychologytoday.com/us/blog/teen-angst/201207/the-dangers-teen-sexting and https://www.sciencedaily.com/releases/2014/02/140220165625.htm.

218 https://www.bound4life.com/history-of-contraception-in-the-protestant-church.

219 https://www.catholic.com/tract/celibacy-and-the-priesthood.

220 https://www.bound4life.com/history-of-contraception-in-the-protestant-church.

221 Ibid.

222 Carlson, 68.

223 Jonathan Eig, *The Birth of the Pill: How Four Crusaders Reinvented Sex and Launched a Revolution*, W.W. Norton & Company. Kindle Edition, 15.

224 Ibid., 16.

225 Carlson, 72.

226 https://www.anglicancommunion.org/media/127728/1908.pdf.

227 https://www.touchstonemag.com/archives/article.php?id=20-04-020-f.

228 Josiah Strong, *The New Era or The Coming Kingdom* (New York: The Baker and Taylor, 1893), 80, quoted at https://en.wikipedia.org/wiki/Josiah_Strong#Works_by_Strong.

229 Ibid., 34–36, 60–72, 80.

230 Strong, *The New Era*, 34–36.

231 Charles Kingsley, "The Natural Theology of the Future" (paper read at Sion College, January 10, 1871) quoted in Amy Laura Hall, *Conceiving Parenthood: American Protestantism and the Spirit of Reproduction* (Grand Rapids: William B. Eerdmans, 2008), 228.

232 Amy Laura Hall, *Conceiving Parenthood: American Protestantism and the Spirit of Reproduction* (Grand Rapids: Eerdmans, 2008), 215.

233 Christine Rosen, *Preaching Eugenics: Religious Leaders and the American Eugenic Movement* (New York: Oxford University Press, 2004), 4.

234 Phillips E. Osgood, "The Refiner's Fire," Eugenics 1 (December 1928): 10–15.

235 Carlson, 94.

236 Margaret Sanger, *The Pivot of Civilization* (Lenox, MA: Hard Press, 2006) 91-92, quoted in Benjamin Wiker, *10 Books that Screwed Up the World* (Washington, DC: Regnery, 2008), 137.

237 Ibid., 17.

238 R. Marie Griffith, *Moral Combat: How Sex Divided American Christians and Fractured American Politics* (New York: Basic Books, 2017), 5.

239 Ibid., 8.

240 Ibid., 8.

241 Sanger wrote to a friend, for example, "The R.C.'s are certainly taking their stand against this subject and me . . . but it may serve to awaken the Protestant element in time to save the country later on." Quoted in McGreevy, 159.

242 Griffith, 33.
243 Allan Carlson, "Sanger's Victory: How Planned Parenthood's Founder Played the Christians—and Won," *Touchstone Magazine*, Jan/Feb 2011, https://www. touchstonemag.com/archives/article.php?id=24-01-039-f.
244 There were Protestant voices that resisted, of course. Evangelist Billy Sunday was a strong opponent of contraception and even said "I am a Catholic" on this question, for example. But the movement within Protestantism was unquestionably toward embracing a new sexual morality.
245 Carlson, *Godly Seed,* 98.
246 Rick Nutt, *The Whole Gospel for the Whole World: Sherwood Eddy and the American Protestant Mission* (Macon, GA: Mercer University Press, 1997), 156.
247 "Dr. Fosdick Urges Birth Rate Control," *New York Times*, December 5, 1927. https://timesmachine.nytimes.com/timesmachine/1927/12/05/95021883. html?pageNumber=30.
248 There are certain "elements" in Scripture, he wrote in 1922, that "are not final; they are always being superseded; revelation is progressive." Harry Fosdick, "Shall the Fundamentalists Win?" A sermon preached on May 21, 1922. http://baptiststudiesonline. com/wp-content/uploads/2007/01/shall-the-fundamentalists-win.pdf.
249 Ibid.
250 Carlson, 99.
251 Carlson, 99.
252 Margaret Sanger, *An Autobiography* (New York: Dover, 1971 [1938]), 410.
253 Lambeth Conference, 1939, Resolution 15.
254 Federal Council of Churches of Christ in America, *Moral Aspects of Birth Control. Some Recent Pronouncements of Religious Bodies* (New York: Federal Council of Churches, 1936).
255 Kathleen A. Tobin, *American Religious Debate over Birth Control,* (Jefferson, NC: McFarland & Company, 2001), 164.
256 Ibid.
257 Alfred Martin Rehwinkel, *Planned Parenthood and Birth Control in the Light of Christian Ethics* (St. Louis, MO: Concordia Publishing House, 1959), 3–5.
258 For a good contemporary example of this line of thinking, see Dennis P. Hollinger, *The Meaning of Sex: Christian Ethics and the Moral Life* (Grand Rapids: Baker, 2009), 165. "As Genesis makes clear, God has granted to humans the role of stewards or caretakers of the created world (cf. Ps. 8:5-8). We are not at the mercy of nature, which is at once a good fit of God but also a fallen reality. As stewards we are decision makers, called to make wise decisions for the glory of God and the good of the world. Humans can and do revert to idolatrous and unethical ways of carrying out God's mandate, but we can legitimately enter into the course of nature, not to change God's designs, but to steward those designs. Moreover, because of the fallenness of our world, we sometimes seek to alter nature to alleviate suffering and pain.
    "Within this framework of stewardship we can accept contraception, not in order to negate the procreative character of sex, but to steward the gifts and resources that God grants to us. We can utilize nonnatural means of contraception to work with nature just as we steward many dimensions of natural life through technology and human knowledge."
259 "Evangelicals Face up to Birth Control Issue," *Christianity Today* 4 (December 21, 1959), 31–32.

260 George Dugan, "Graham Sees Hope in Birth Control," *New York Times* (December 13, 1959). https://timesmachine.nytimes.com/timesmachine/1959/12/13/88912268. html?pageNumber=49.

261 For the fuller story, see Mary Eberstadt, *Adam and Eve After the Pill* (San Francisco: Ignatius, 2012) and my documentary film *Unprotected: The Untold Story of the Sexual Revolution*.

262 https://www.bound4life.com/history-of-contraception-in-the-protestant-church.

263 Ibid.

264 John Warwick Montgomery, "How to Decide the Birth Control Question" *Christianity Today*, March 4, 1966. https://www.christianitytoday.com/ct/1966/march-4/how-to-decide-birth-control-question.html.

265 Ibid.

266 Using natural law simply doesn't work, Montgomery claims, because humans take control of "natural" phenomena all the time, and it is perfectly moral to do so. We shave the hair off of our faces and harvest vegetation; how is it any different to take control of our fertility? https://www.christianitytoday.com/ct/1966/march-4/how-to-decide-birth-control-question.html. This is a straw-man argument that badly misunderstands natural law and misrepresents the Catholic argument from it.

267 For example, *Christianity Today* would later reference this work as the evangelical alternative to *Humanae Vitae*. https://www.christianitytoday.com/ct/1968/november-8/old-testament-and-birth-control.html.

268 Bruce K. Waltke, "The Old Testament and Birth Control," *Christianity Today*, November 8, 1968. https://www.christianitytoday.com/ct/1968/november-8/old-testament-and-birth-control.html.

269 Ibid.

270 "Evangelical Scholars Endorse Birth Control" *Christianity Today*, September 27, 1968. https://www.christianitytoday.com/ct/1968/september-27/evangelical-scholars-endorse-birth-control.html.

271 "Southern Baptists Approve Abortion in Certain Cases," *New York Times*, June 3, 1971, 43, available at https://www.nytimes.com/1971/06/03/archives/southern-baptists-approve-abortion-in-certain-cases.html.

272 David Roach, "How Southern Baptists became pro-life," *Baptist Press*, January 16, 2015, available at https://www.baptistpress.com/resource-library/news/how-southern-baptists-became-pro-life/. (Criswell later changed his view and became an opponent of abortion.)

273 Carlson, 140.

274 McGreevy, 262.

275 http://www.nrlc.org/uploads/communications/stateofabortion2022.pdf.

276 *The Mike Wallace Interviews*, September 21, 1957, transcript and video available at https://hrc.contentdm.oclc.org/digital/collection/p15878coll90/id/27/.

277 Leslie Woodstock Tentler, *Catholics and Contraception: An American History* (Ithaca, NY: Cornell University Press, 2004), 40.

278 McGreevy, 161.

279 Ibid.

280 McGreevy, 223.

281 We won't take time to tell that story here, but there are several good resources, including McGreevy, chapter 8, "Life."

282 Tentler, 189.

283 Ibid.

284 Ibid.

285 For example, see Tentler, 204.

286 "Widening Crack in the Wall of Catholicism" in the editorial "Missing Notes in Theology" *Christianity Today*, September 27, 1968.

287 *New York Times*, July 31, 1968.

288 Christopher West, "From Humanae Vitae to Theology of the Body" https://ccli. org/2018/07/from-humanae-vitae-to-theology-of-the-body/.

289 Ibid.

290 Maura Judkis, "Helen Gurley Brown: 'To be desired sexually . . . is about the best thing there is.'" *Washington Post*, August 14, 2012. https://www.washingtonpost.com/blogs/ arts-post/post/helen-gurley-brown-to-be-desired-sexually-is-about-the-best-thing-there-is/2012/08/13/b5c70ada-e584-11e1-8741-940e3f6dbf48_blog.html.

291 See also https://www.statista.com/statistics/276025/us-percentage-of-births-to-unmarried-women/.

292 https://www.nytimes.com/2011/05/26/us/26marry.html.

293 https://www.pewresearch.org/social-trends/2019/11/06/the-landscape-of-marriage-and-cohabitation-in-the-u-s/#fn-26820-4.

294 For firsthand stories about the effects of divorce, I recommend Leila Miller, *Primal Loss: The Now-Adult Children of Divorce Speak* (Phoenix: LCB Publishing, 2017).

295 https://www.nytimes.com/2012/01/21/us/more-protestants-oppose-birth-control. html see also http://www.leaderu.com/ftissues/ft9812/articles/contraception.html.

296 https://matthewvines.tumblr.com/post/19110639328/the-gay-debate-the-bible-and homosexuality.

297 https://www.nytimes.com/2012/09/16/fashion/matthew-vines-wont-rest-in-defending-gay-christians.html?pagewanted=all&_r=0.

298 Matthew Vines, *God and the Gay Christian: The Biblical Case in Support of Same Sex Relationships* (New York: Convergent, 2014).

299 Albert Mohler, "God, the Gospel, and the Gay Challenge—A Response to Matthew Vines" https://albertmohler.com/2014/04/22/god-the-gospel-and-the-gay-challenge-a-response-to-matthew-vines.

300 https://reformationproject.org/resources/.

301 https://press.vatican.va/content/salastampa/en/bollettino/ pubblico/2021/03/15/210315b.html.

302 The beginning of the transgender phenomenon, in which there has been an exponential increase in trans-identifying youth, is generally dated to the announcement by Bruce Jenner in April 2015 that he had changed his name to Caitlyn and would henceforth be "identifying" as a woman.

303 For a good survey of what is happening in the culture regarding transgenderism, see Abigail Shrier, *Irreversible Damage: The Transgender Craze Seducing Our Daughters* (Washington, D.C., Regnery Publishing, 2020) as well as my documentary film *Dysconnected: The Real Story Behind the Transgender Explosion.*

304 Eliel Cruz, "Where in the Bible does it say you can't be transgender? Nowhere." *The Washington Post*, August 26, 2016 https://www.washingtonpost.com/news/acts-of-faith/ wp/2016/08/26/where-in-the-bible-does-it-say-you-cant-be-transgender-nowhere/.

305 Ibid.

306 Ibid.

307 See, for example, Focus on the Family's explanation for why they uphold traditional

morality regarding transgenderism at https://www.focusonthefamily.com/get-help/transgenderism-our-position/.

308 Cruz.

309 https://www.hrc.org/resources/what-does-the-bible-say-about-transgender-people

310 Ibid.

311 https://twitter.com/NeoPagliacci/status/1529848090009686016.

312 Mark Wingfield, "Why Being Transgender is not a sin", November 9, 2018 https://baptistnews.com/article/why-being-transgender-is-not-a-sin/#.YpERXy1h1mA

313 See "The Church's Position on Transgenderism" at https://www.catholic.com/qa/the-churchs-position-on-transgenderism-0.

314 The link between transgenderism and pedophilia is clear when you examine the history of the movement, including the lives of men such as John Kinsey and John Money. As for transhumanism's relationship to transgenderism, see, for example, Martine Rothblatt, *From Transgender to Transhuman: A Manifesto on the Freedom of Form* (Martine Rothblatt Publishing: 2011) Rothblatt, a biological male who identifies as female, is a very influential tech inventor and CEO who has invested huge amounts of time and money in trans activism. For more on both of these subjects, see my documentary *Dysconnected: The Real Story Behind the Transgender Explosion.*

315 For example, in May of 2022, Archbishop Salvatore Cordileone of San Francisco announced that House Speaker Nancy Pelosi could not receive the Eucharist in his archdiocese on account of her pro-abortion policies. He wrote that a "Catholic legislator who supports procured abortion, after knowing the teaching of the Church, commits a manifestly grave sin which is a cause of most serious scandal to others." As such, she was "not to be admitted to Holy Communion, until such time as you publicly repudiate your advocacy for the legitimacy of abortion and confess and receive absolution of this grave sin in the sacrament of Penance."